Garden Design Ideas

THE BEST OF
FINE GARDENING

Garden Design Ideas

The Taunton Press

Cover photo: Rosalind Loeb Wanke

Back-cover photos: left, bottom center and top right,
Susan Kahn; top center, Mark Kane;
bottom right, Nancy Beaubaire

Taunton
BOOKS & VIDEOS
for fellow enthusiasts

© 1994 by The Taunton Press, Inc.
All rights reserved.

First printing: March 1994
Second printing: January 1996
Printed in the United States of America

A FINE GARDENING Book

FINE GARDENING® is a trademark of The Taunton Press, Inc.,
registered in the U.S. Patent and Trademark Office.

The Taunton Press
63 South Main Street
Box 5506
Newtown, CT 06470-5506

Library of Congress Cataloging-in-Publication Data

Garden design ideas.
        p.   cm. — (The Best of fine gardening)
    Articles originally published in Fine gardening magazine.
    "A Fine gardening book"— T.p. verso.
    Includes index.
    ISBN 1-56158-079-1
    1. Gardens — Design. 2. Landscape gardening.
    I. Fine gardening. II. Series.
SB473.G2883   1994   93-41876
712'.6 — dc20   CIP

Contents

Introduction

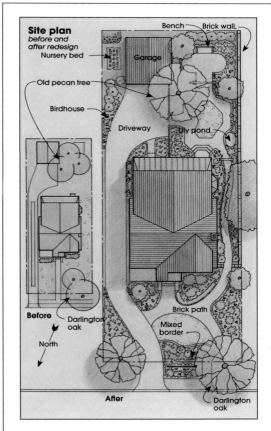

Site plan
before and after redesign

Nursery bed

Bench — Brick wall

Garage

Old pecan tree

Birdhouse

Driveway

Lily pond

Before

Darlington oak

North

Brick path

Mixed border

After

Darlington oak

Here are the best of the garden-design articles presented by *Fine Gardening* magazine in its first five years of publication.

In this beautifully illustrated collection, landscape architects, designers and home gardeners explain the principles of design and describe gardens in which they have been successfully applied. Among the articles, you'll find concrete guidelines for all aspects of garden making, from drawing a map to deciding on a style, from shaping a garden room to laying out paths. Ranging from the tried-and-true to the innovative, many of the approaches recommended by the authors are sure to suit your property.

You'll find the articles in this collection especially helpful and inspiring because they are the work of enthusiasts, gardeners who have given much thought to designing their properties and want to help you enjoy the process of shaping your garden too. Sharing their hard-won experience, the authors tell you the problems they faced, what they wanted from their gardens and how they combined existing features with new plants and structures to achieve their goals.

The editors of *Fine Gardening* hope you'll experiment with the ideas in this collection of articles. No matter which you choose to try, your efforts will be rewarded.

"The Best of *Fine Gardening*" series collects articles from back issues of *Fine Gardening* magazine. A note on p. 96 gives the date of first publication for each article; product availability, suppliers' addresses and prices may have changed since then. Other books in the series include *Perennials, Shrubs & Trees* and *Great Gardens.*

Here are five design rules at work together. Along with a path for the eye (the first rule of design), there is a focal point (the distant fence and chair), a background, a controlled range of colors (mostly greens, blues and reds, with accents of yellow), and lots of texture.

Principles of Design
Follow these five rules and get impressive results

by Robert Smaus

Exactly what is it that makes a garden look good? Are there rules or principles that govern the design of gardens? It may sound bold, but I am convinced there are five: provide a path for the eye; build a background; find a focal point; control color; and add texture.

These rules are not arbitrary, nor are they my invention. As Garden Editor for the *Los Angeles Times*, I have been privileged to see a great many gardens and to meet a great many garden designers and landscape architects. They have suggested these rules; all I have done is organize and simplify.

Have I made them too simple? I don't think so. Of course, all rules can be broken, sometimes with exciting results. But to break a rule, you must first know and understand it. Look at any favorite garden, even a photograph of one, and see if there is a path for the eye, a good background, a focal point. I'm sure there is. The rules can be elaborated on endlessly, so no two gardens need ever look alike.

These principles will help you plan a new garden thoughtfully, or rethink an old garden—not only are they rules, they are a sort of checklist and recipe. Put them to use. Look at your own garden and check them off. If you discover why some part of the garden has been bothering you, you won't be alone. I know the rules have helped me countless times. They greatly simplify the sometimes numbing complexity of design.

Provide a path for the eye.

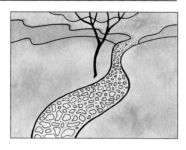

Try to see a path as "the tracks the eye rides upon," as Hugh Johnson has so neatly put it in "The Principles of Gardening" (Simon and Schuster, New York). Too often, the paths through a garden are an afterthought. They should be the first thought. A path guides the eye through the garden as though the eye were riding on rails. Only later does the path guide the feet. Lawns or clearings can be paths, but they work better as destinations. They tend to lack direction, so the eye wanders, looking for something to settle on.

Paths must appear to lead somewhere, and the further the better. In garden design, the shortest distance between two points is not always the best place for a path. On the average piece of property, you simply can't wander very far, so it's not too important if a path really gets you somewhere. It is better to prolong that all-too-short journey, making the garden seem much larger than it is, satisfying a craving shared by most gardeners for a little more acreage. Japanese gardens often contain tortuous paths. Although the paths can seem designed to trip you up, in fact they're meant to slow you down so you notice what's around you.

Paths give a garden focus and structure. A strong path tells you where to look. Along the way you discover the other parts of a garden. First decide where the path is to go, and the other elements of a garden will begin to fall into place.

Build a background.

Once the eye has followed a path to its end and is free to roam, it needs guiding. The background helps by obscuring what might be distracting and objectionable—a telephone pole or a neighbor's tool shed, for instance—and by emphasizing what is nice. The background itself, be it fence or foliage, is not what you should be looking at. It is there to make other things look good, to focus attention on the flowers, or the fish pond—to make them stand out.

The best backgrounds are rather plain. They might be fences, walls, shrubs or trees, and they are often a combination of these elements. Fences and walls take up the least space but make a rather abrupt boundary for

the garden. Planting shrubs in front of them, at least in some places, softens them. Shrubs, all by themselves, are perhaps the best background for a garden because they look more like an edge than an end. Rather than stating emphatically, "this is the end of the garden," as a fence does, shrubs hint that there might be more beyond. This illusion vanishes, however, if shrubs are planted too much in a row, at the very edge of the garden; then they become too wall-like themselves.

The background for the garden does not have to be as far back as is physically possible. Lining up shrubs along the property line may enclose the garden so abruptly that it feels smaller than it should. Let the background weave in and out along the property line so it makes a soft edge for the garden, and you will be less aware that there is an edge.

To get some idea of what needs hiding and what doesn't, sketch a view of the garden (from the back door, for instance). Or photograph the garden, have prints made, and then draw right on the prints with a grease pencil. Hide what you don't like with sketched-in trees or shrubs.

Though one scene may be the most looked-at (from

Build a background. A fence or an informal hedge sets off the ornamental features of the garden while hiding distractions that lie beyond the property line. Here, both fence and hedge dramatize a swath of flowers.

Illustrations: Lainé Roundy

the kitchen window, for instance), gardens have many views. When you have sketched what the garden will look like from inside of the house, walk outdoors and look back toward the house to see if perhaps that view could be improved.

Find a focal point.

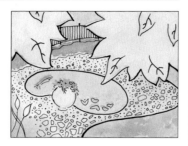

A focal point is the final resting place for the eye, once the eye has followed the path and been halted by the background. The focal point should be interesting and fairly obvious. In my dry California garden, the focal point is a large urn filled with aquatic plants, fed by a burbling fountain that makes it even easier to spot. Traditional focal points include sculpture, furniture and even bird feeders, but a particularly distinctive or colorful plant can also be the focus of attention.

A focal point should beckon. The clever designer chooses something that is intriguing and attracts attention, but which cannot be completely appreciated at a distance. Generally, the focal point should beckon from the far end of a garden, so it draws you nearer. Along the path can be other, lesser focal points that lead the way, much like landing lights along an airfield or clumps of wildflowers along a mountain trail.

Control color.

This is really tough. Flowers are too pretty to say no to, but some must be refused admittance to a well-designed garden, at least until you've gained experience with color. It is possible to have an attractive garden with a riotous mix of colors, but only if you provide a plain background and other strong elements to give the garden structure. And no one color should dominate. If you find color a confusing subject (we men have a particularly difficult time since we have so little experience with color), try simple schemes at first and then add to them as your confidence grows.

Gardeners have discovered that you can divide flowers into two groups—those that are colored red through blue, and those that are yellow through orange. If you plant flowers from only one group, you simplify the color scheme without detracting much from the garden's allure, since the colors in each group generally harmonize.

There is a trick—the reds must be pure, or tinged with blue. If there's a hint of orange or yellow, reds turn hot and move into the other group of colors. Be particularly careful with red roses—they can go either way, toward orange or pink. Pink is probably the most common color in the red-through-blue group, and a very easy color to live with in the garden. There are hundreds of pink flowers, and you can even slide toward salmon without upsetting the color cart.

Flowers in the red-through-blue range are particularly pleasing because their colors tend to look cool and comfortable. They show up best in cool light—under overcast

Find a focal point. A garden needs at least one focal point—a feature that attracts the eye and lures you nearer. Here, a birdbath and a trio of rocks provide the focal point for a quiet corner of photographer Kathlene Persoff's garden in Los Angeles, designed in part by Christine Rosmini.

Control color. Subtly harmonious colors help a garden's other features to shine. Cool colors predominate here: blues and reds in the flowers, gray in the flagstones and silver in the lamb's-ears and artemisia behind the urn.

skies for instance, or in the spring, before the sun climbs to its summer zenith.

Yellow and orange are hot colors and are harder to handle than reds and blues, but they are invaluable in summer when paler, more pastel colors almost disappear in the bright sunlight. Bright yellows and oranges do not mix easily with other colors, so they are often used alone. Subtler yellows and oranges will blend in if they are kept in the minority. Yellow contrasts dramatically with violet or purple flowers, and strong yellow and orange flowers can make an exciting accent in an otherwise red-blue garden. With time you can discover how to use both groups of colors in the same bed, though one group should always be decidedly dominant.

Developing satisfying color schemes can become the lifework of a gardener (along with learning how to grow the particular plants that one needs to create these schemes, for just any plant won't do). In smaller gardens, color is often the biggest part of garden planning. Once those paths are in, the background is planted, and the beds for the flowers are in place, we could just sit back and watch things grow if it weren't for trying to get the colors right.

Add texture.

By texture I mean all the rest—the details and the big things, plants tucked here and there, pebbles and rocks strategically placed, benches and patios—everything that fleshes out a garden.

Texture is best left for last. If this strikes you as rather odd (leaving the placement of a patio until last), consider that the right location may not appear until the paths and backgrounds and flower beds are in place. Perhaps there is one spot from which the beds look best; that's where the patio should go. And there's no rule that says the patio must be by the house. That's simply convention.

It's important to pay attention to the texture of certain things. Nothing destroys the harmony of a garden quicker than too great a variety of man-made textures. For instance, avoid a mixture of paving materials. If you start with flagstone, finish with flagstone—don't add a patio of concrete and a brick wall.

With plants, though, the more texture the merrier, as long as the most dramatic are used as accents and do not overpower the rest of the garden. Go out of your way to look for plants with shiny leaves, fuzzy leaves, rumpled leaves.

Adding texture, like playing with color, never ends. Years after a garden is "finished," you can find places and ways to add detail, and age will add it's own patina to the well-planned garden. ☐

Robert Smaus is Garden Editor of the Los Angeles Times *and gardens in Los Angeles.*

Add texture. Texture enlivens the garden. Here it takes many forms: shrubs, cactus, water plants, flagstones, urns and ornaments.

A Map for Garden Design

Site analysis probes the possibilities of your property

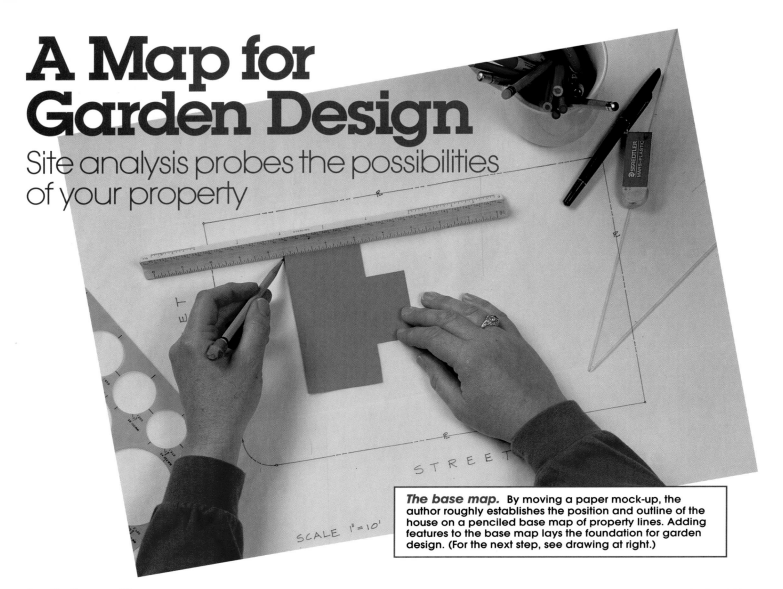

The base map. By moving a paper mock-up, the author roughly establishes the position and outline of the house on a penciled base map of property lines. Adding features to the base map lays the foundation for garden design. (For the next step, see drawing at right.)

by Cathyann Plumer

Understanding your whole property before you ever pick up a spade—where the sun shines in summer, where water pools after a rain, where the wind is fierce in winter—can help you create a garden that makes the most of your site. The shrub borders can be placed to hide eyesores; plants can be matched to soil, sun and drainage; the eye can be directed toward good views; and the flower beds can enhance the views from inside the house.

As a landscape architect, I inventory a property and draw a detailed map before I ever start sketching designs. In the language of my profession, I do a site analysis. To prepare a site analysis, you map every physical feature and condition of your property. Some of the things you need to know are simple—how close to a property line you may build a gazebo or a 6-ft. fence; the location of your septic system, well or water line. Other issues are more complex—restrictions on development of a wetlands area or the flow of runoff across your property. Let's start at the beginning.

Look for existing maps first

The first step usually involves a visit to town or county offices to look for maps of your property. Because each state is organized differently, I can't give you the precise office where you can find the information you need. I recommend that you start by visiting the local clerk or the planning, zoning, or building office and asking the personnel there to steer you to the correct office. Ask for surveys that show the boundaries and topography (ground contours) of your property. You should also ask for any other maps on record. They may cover soil surveys, legal easements, wetlands areas, watercourses, ponds, buildings, and other natural or man-made features. You usually can buy copies for a small fee.

Research all regulations pertaining to your property. These might include zoning regulations, wetlands regulations, special development area regulations, deed restrictions, condominium association regulations, and other municipal and state ordinances.

After you obtain all the information you can, decide if it is sufficient. If you are building an addition to your house and are unsure of boundaries, a new survey may be necessary. But if you are trying to site a shrub border or shade trees well away from the property line, you need less precise detail.

The topographic accuracy you need depends on your land and what projects you are undertaking. If you anticipate moving a driveway, adding an in-ground swimming pool, or undertaking any other major construction

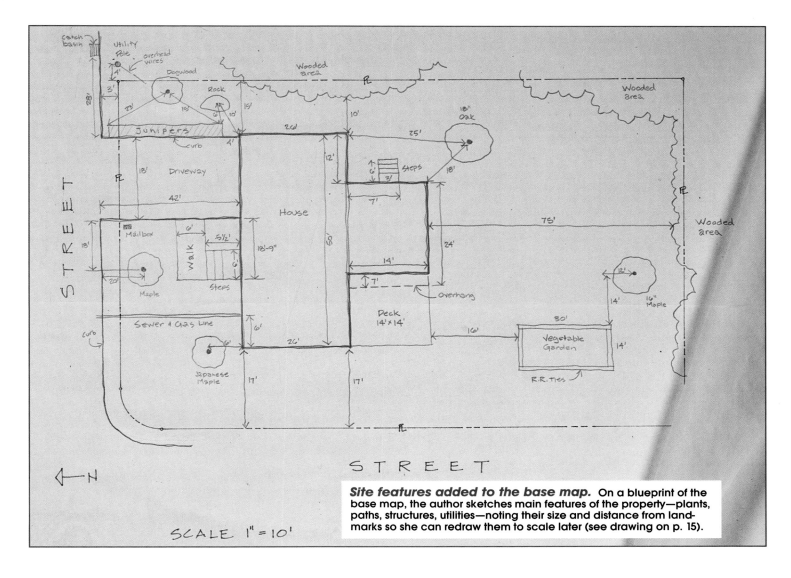

Site features added to the base map. On a blueprint of the base map, the author sketches main features of the property—plants, paths, structures, utilities—noting their size and distance from landmarks so she can redraw them to scale later (see drawing on p. 15).

SCALE 1" = 10'

requiring significant site grading, the accuracy of the topographic map is very important, and you may want to hire a surveyor. If you plan simply to break ground for new beds and borders, you can just estimate ground contours with simple measurements.

Step one: make the base map

The next step is to combine what you've gleaned into one drawing— the "base map" in the lingo of my profession. If you've collected several maps, they're likely to be drawn at different scales, so you will have to redraw them to one scale.

Keep your base map a reasonable size—no more than 24 in. × 36 in.— and choose a suitable scale for the dimensions of your property. Common site scales for residential properties are: 1 in. = 10 ft.; 1 in. = 20 ft., and 1 in. = 40 ft. Use an engineering scale, which looks like a three-sided ruler; it helps you measure off distances on a map quickly. The boundary map

in town records is likely to be at a smaller scale than you'll need. To transfer it, extend the original lot lines on the new scale one at a time, starting with straight lines first. Saving curved lines for last makes the job a little easier.

Draw the base map on tracing vellum or Mylar so it can be reproduced as often as needed on blueprints or photocopies. Vellum is a special drafting paper, and Mylar is a film of translucent plastic. Both are long-lasting and available at stationery or art stores that sell drafting supplies.

Keep the base map simple. Include only the boundary lines (without all the bearings and distances), as much topography as you need, watercourses, wetlands areas, and a north arrow. Show setback lines—how far buildings must be from property lines. Add buildings, if you can. Be sure to note the scale of the map. When the base map is finished, have a photocopy or blueprint made.

Step two: add main features

The next task is to map the main features of your property, such as the house (if you didn't know its exact location before), driveway, paths or sidewalks, tool sheds or garage, outdoor faucets and electric outlets. Note overhead or buried power lines; your septic tank and its field; your well, the pipes to and from the house or the municipal water, and sewer pipes. Note ponds or streams, large or important trees, rock outcroppings and similar features.

If your base map does not show the house, take field measurements and plot it on the base map before taking other measurements. Measure the house and draw it to scale on a separate piece of paper. Then locate the house on the base map by using distances to other points—a utility pole, the edge of the street, a fence along a property line, or even a drainage structure in the road. Check the final location from all sides for relative accuracy. Let any minor inaccuracy fall on the least critical side, farthest from all property lines.

Take the copy of your base map outdoors and note site features and field measurements directly on it. You will need a helper, a 50-ft. or 100-ft. cloth or metal tape, a large clipboard for the map and a note pad. Use well-identified features on the base map—the house, utility poles, the road—for your starting points. Accuracy decreases rapidly when measuring distances longer than the length of your tape measure, so keep all your measured distances reasonably short. Also remember to hold the tape measure level at all times. To be accurate, site survey measurements must be horizontal, not parallel to the ground. On a slope, your helper may have to hold the tape measure at ground level while you hold the other end overhead.

Techniques for measuring and sketching depend on what you are recording. Some features, such as woodlands, lawns, front walks and long, sweeping driveways require you to make only a few basic measurements such as distance from the house or length and width. Then, working from the key points (such as the house location), you sketch the overall shape on the base map. Other site features, such as pools, buildings, and patios, will have shapes that can be measured and drawn fairly easily.

Your field sketches do not have to be highly accurate, but you must be sure to record dimensions and distances completely so you can redraw site features to scale later. Reviewing the measurements can also help you catch field mistakes.

Indoors, transfer all your field information to the original vellum. This is now your final base map. Make copies of it for the next step. (Always work from copies for site analysis and design. It allows you to pursue and evaluate several different methods of creating your ideal landscape.)

Step three: add gardening conditions

Now that you have mapped the physical features of your property, it is time to take careful note of the remaining factors that will affect your garden—sun, shade, views, access, traffic and more. Take a copy of your final base map with you, walk the property and take notes. Take photos, too; they'll refresh your memory later. It's also helpful to have photos from several seasons. Here are some of the features to look for and record:

Plants—Note everything that grows, how it looks and its use. Look at the condition of beds, lawns, shrubs and trees. You may hate the scraggly shrubs that came with the place, but note them, because they have to come out before anything better can replace them. Note wildlife habitats and the quality of wooded areas.

Condition of main features—Look closely at the condition of paths, walks, fences and other structures. Note if the sidewalk is full of cracks or the old arbor is charming but leaning precariously under the weight of vines.

Access—Is the main entrance to the house obvious to visitors? Where do visitors park? Is the driveway easy or impossible to negotiate?

Traffic patterns—Note how people get to the house, porch, patio, garage and basement. What route do you take when you're laden with groceries? How do you get the compost from the pile to the garden? Where is the lawn worn out because of heavy foot traffic? Have the neighborhood kids created a shortcut across the property? Is there a path to the storage shed that appears logical but tends to be treacherous?

Sun and shade—The sun is higher in the sky and rises farther north in summer than it does in spring, fall or winter. The difference is dramatic in Minnesota, less in southern Texas. Areas in full sun in June might be shaded at other times of the year. Take photos and observations from several points on the property (in all four seasons, if possible) to learn exactly where shadows fall. A manual on passive solar construction can help you map sun lines.

Slopes—Problems increase as the slope does. A vertical drop of 5 ft. over 100 horizontal feet is gentle (5%) and poses few problems. Drops of 25 ft. or more over 100 ft. (25%) limit your options severely. Erosion, for example, becomes more of an issue as the grade becomes steeper. If you rip out a lawn on a slope that is too steep to mow comfortably, a downpour on exposed soil could wash away newly-planted groundcover plants. Note slopes and their percentage grades on your base map so you can evaluate projects later.

Also, note the orientation of slopes. A cold, north-facing slope offers a very different environment for plants than a warm, south-facing one does.

Drainage—Note spots where water tends to collect for quite a while after a rain or that stay wet in spring long after the rest of the yard is dry and workable. There are desirable plants that can stand wet feet, but some favorites, such as junipers, may not survive a single winter in a damp location. If you want to install a concrete or lined pool, the lowest spot on the property is the wrong place to put it—runoff will overfill it since there's no place else for excess water to go. A natural pond with an earth bottom, however, can act as a collector and should go in a low, naturally wet area.

Wind—Summer breezes are welcome, but winter gales, particularly in combination with winter sun, may dry out and kill broad-leaved evergreens or conifers. Note any locations exposed to winter wind. You might want to plant hardy trees or shrubs as windbreaks for more sensitive plants.

Trees—Mature trees are an asset to any property, but they limit what you can grow nearby. Note the species of any tree, recording the approximate diameter of its trunk and canopy spread. You need this information so you can avoid making garden plans that might kill the tree with too much planting or trenching. (For more information on gardening around tree roots, see *FG* #26, pp. 58-61.)

Views—Note both the good views and the eyesores on your property and beyond. Look from inside the house and from outside. Record what you see out the window when you are having your morning coffee. Is there a wonderful view of trees or mountains or water? Is there a lousy view of the back of the neighbor's garage or a chain-link dog-run? What is the view from the porch or deck? Note the span of views on your map—a single arrow or an arc, depending on size. Also note the distance to the eyesore. If it's near, you may have to plant trees to obscure it; if farther away, a couple of large shrubs may be enough to soften your view.

Soil type—If you have located a soil survey in your research, note your soil type. If there is no survey, poke

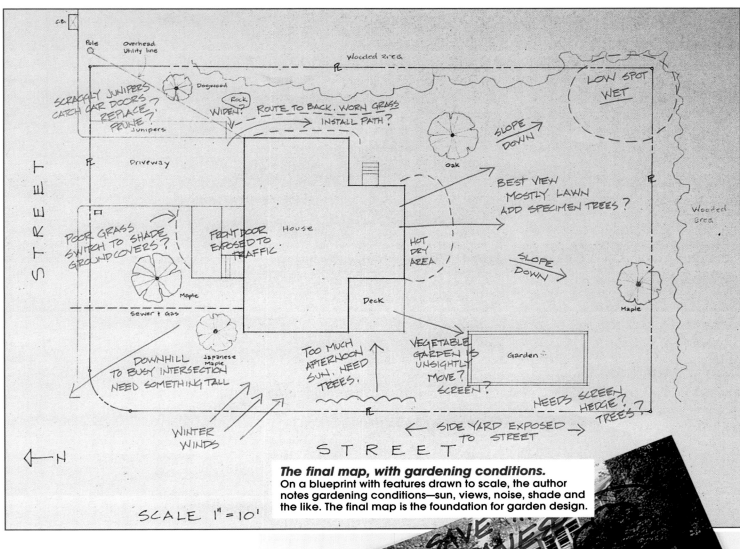

SCALE 1" = 10'

The final map, with gardening conditions.
On a blueprint with features drawn to scale, the author notes gardening conditions—sun, views, noise, shade and the like. The final map is the foundation for garden design.

around in various spots. Feel a handful of soil. Is it rocky? granular? slimy? State Cooperative Extension Services usually offer a soil testing service that will describe the composition of your soil. Knowing your soil will help you select suitable trees and shrubs, or prepare you to amend beds for annuals and perennials that require different soil to thrive.

The next step

After you have recorded all the features of your property onto a copy of the base map, the fun part begins. You are ready to start designing. With your site analysis in hand, you can check your daydreams against the limits and constraints of your property. Now let your imagination run and see how you can make the best of your opportunities. □

Cathyann Plumer of Monroe, Connecticut, is a member of the American Society of Landscape Architects.

The author makes notes on her snapshots to help fill out the final map (shown above).

On the path to the past: the author sketched the journey that he and his childhood friends made to reach their favorite place, a secret pond in a distant woods. Here, behind the house, they cross an orchard and vegetable garden. By recalling the journey and his favorite place, the author found inspiration for his garden.

The First Step in Garden Design

Exploring memories of favorite places for inspiration

by Will Hooker

Designing a garden can be terribly frustrating. Faced with too few or too many choices, do you have to wait for the lightning bolt of creative inspiration? Where do the ideas come from?

I recommend that you look back for inspiration, back to the places you remember most fondly, the venues of happy, cherished experiences. Recalling favorite places can reveal hidden landscape preferences. It is also extremely enjoyable.

Childhood holds a treasure of favorite places. I've found that the most significant ones are those we knew during leaps of growth, or moments of passage. In childhood, we seemed to see more clearly, taking things as they were. We were also physically closer to the earth, so sights, smells and everyday objects seemed bigger, richer and more significant. Innocent and unable to easily distinguish between fantasy and reality, we felt that Grandma's garden was alive and full of magic. Our memories of those favorite childhood locations may serve as unconscious standards against which we measure all other places for the rest of our lives.

I often help gardeners explore their childhood memories for design inspiration. The method I use has three parts. The first step is to put yourself in a meditative, dreamy frame of mind. Then you search your past for favorite places, pick one, and return to it in imagination, reliving the moments you spent there. Finally, you ask yourself what you liked most about the site and how you could recreate a similar effect in your garden.

Personal memories

I first recalled my own favorite places in a seminar at North Carolina State University in the late 1970s. Randy Hester, a professor in the Department of Landscape Architecture, gathered a group of students to study landscape values. In order to help future clients, we sought to uncover what we valued. We each looked through our past and chose ten memorable places. We drew plans and sketches and wrote short descriptions of these places. Then we analyzed the sites and tried to categorize their elements.

The most special place from my childhood was a small, hidden pool in a woodlot about a half-mile behind my home in up-state New York. My brother and I and our neighborhood buddies discovered the pool one summer day when I was about ten. When I drew images of the trip from the back of my house through the fields and woods to the pool, I discovered, to my surprise, that those 28 sketches revealed most of my landscape biases. For example, I have difficulty designing woodland landscapes.

A mysterious world lures the author and his friends into the woods. They shinny up saplings and ride the tops to the ground.

In one of my sketches, my friends and I are passing the vegetable garden that provided most of my family's food. Looking at the sketch, I realized that I am not comfortable with a property that lacks sun and the capacity to grow large quantities of produce. I also realized that as I've moved around, I've gardened at those homes that had good sun, interspersing vegetables, herbs and fruit trees among the ornamentals. But when I've had to live on a shady lot, I've ignored the grounds and treated the house as only a temporary place to eat and sleep.

My memories of the trip to the woodland pool also explained why I love wild fields. Behind my childhood home, my parents once planted corn, hoping to attract pheasants that could be taken for the table. They could never bring themselves to shoot those beautiful birds, so they just let the field go. For 15 years, I grew up with that field. I chased

butterflies, tried to salt birds' tails, secretly helped the milkweed spread its children and watched the field turn into a budding young forest. Ever since, abandoned fields and other such transitional places have been dear to my heart; they remind me of the almost magical resilience and vitality of nature.

But the woodland pool had the most dramatic effect on me. I recall one day above all. We were exploring a new part of the woods, doing all the things typical of rowdy ten-year-old boys: shouting, jumping over logs and shinnying up maple saplings to throw ourselves out into space for the thrill of riding the young trees arching to the ground. After several hours, we were tired and thirsty. We looked for our usual sources of water: hollows filled with ground water. We spotted a pool, raced forward, flung ourselves down on the mossy banks and drank deeply of the clear, brownish water. Quenched, we silently sat back, each lost in our private thoughts. Being still for the first time ever in the woods, we heard the insects chatter. Surprisingly, the wind rustling through the tops of the tall hemlocks sounded like waves. The trees seemed to shine, and the woods came alive. The distant hum of autos was our only connection to the outside world. We felt accepted, part of the woodland, part of nature. We talked about it after a while and discovered that we had all experienced the same reverie. We consecrated the spot "Peaceful Valley" and swore a solemn oath of adolescence to never fight there, to never swear there, nor to do anything to disturb the tranquility of that now-sacred spot. Today, to escape the bustle of urban

living, I still seek such enchanted places over all others. They reinforce my connection to nature and bring my life back into perspective.

Designing your own favorite place

You can recall and use favorite places of your own. The first step is to find a quiet spot where you won't be interrupted. Make yourself comfortable and take time to relax. Breathe calmly and try to set your mood to a safe, warm, happy glow. Without thinking of specific places, simply observe the images that come to mind. Often, the first place you see is important, so linger there, examine it, remember everything you can. Imagine now that you are in your favorite play space. Gently hold that image and with your mind's eye, look it over carefully. Move through the image and do again the things you did there as a child. Then return from your memories and sketch the places. Make notes, if necessary, to capture the details. I recommend you try to remember three or more favorite places. The more you remember, the better your chances of finding common elements.

Before you can use a favorite place in garden design, you have to study it carefully. Begin with its structure. All spaces consist of a ground plane, side planes and an overhead plane. Was your favorite place wide or narrow, open to the sky or closed in? If there were trees above, was the canopy high or were there branches just overhead, making the space more intimate? If your property and your favorite place are very different in scale and structure, don't be discouraged. One of my fellow students years ago recalled a favorite seat among tree roots atop a cliff that overlooked a vast panorama. He could evoke the same feeling in a garden with nothing more than a slightly elevated perch.

Study the central feature of your favorite place. If it was water, note its qualities. Was it flowing water or still? If it was still, was it calm or was its surface constantly moving with ripples? The pond in "Peaceful Valley" was enclosed by woods, so the water was always still and reflective.

Once your favorite place is firmly in mind, you can test how its space and features might fit into your landscape. I highly recommend experimenting at full scale. For example, lay out the shape of a pool using a garden hose to

Tired and thirsty, they drink from a secret pond (above). In the lull that follows, the boys fall silent and feel the spell of sheltering hemlocks and still water (right). Inspired by these memories, the author is planning an intimate pond for his garden.

mark the bank. I know gardeners who draw their designs on the yard with powdered lime. If they want to change the design or build it, they simply erase it by raking the lawn or the earth. You can also experiment in three dimensions. If your design extends into the lawn, skip mowing for a few weeks and then carve the shape you want in the tall grass. To evaluate larger features, lash bamboo poles or tomato stakes in the desired shapes and then stand back to take a look. Fill in voids with your mind's eye or with your extended hands. Be certain to look at mock-ups from different places around the yard, inside the house and even out in the street. It also helps, if you can stand it, to leave the mock-ups in place for at least several days so you can see them with fresh eyes at various times.

There's no water where I live today, but I'm planning a pool. The space is small and close to a road, so it won't be as remote as "Peaceful Valley." I'll enclose it on three sides with lattice, however, and cover that with thick vines. To one side of the pool, I'll create a moss-covered mound. Perhaps I'll plant a Canada hemlock and a birch tree just outside the enclosure. One day, when there's a lull in the traffic, I'll sit by the pool and listen to the wind sounding surprisingly like waves as it blows gently through the trees…. Heaven.

Recalling favorite places can inspire garden designs that abound in memories and feelings. Perhaps you'll create a magic place both for yourself and for a child who will one day recall it with grateful delight. □

Will Hooker is a landscape architect and an associate professor of landscape horticulture at North Carolina State University in Raleigh, North Carolina.

Getting Started on a Landscape Design

First steps for a beginner

by David Lee Drotar

Editor's note: Formulating an overall plan for an unlandscaped property can be an overwhelming prospect, even for an experienced gardener. When David Lee Drotar bought his first property two years ago, he'd grown a lot of plants, but he was a novice at design. He's since developed a cohesive and attractive landscape plan that reflects his tastes and needs. We think his account of how he did it will be helpful. To highlight the method that underlies his thinking, we've added the comments that appear in boxes on pp. 20 and 23.

Author Drotar's house and the surrounding unlandscaped property, carved out of former farmland, offered him much opportunity for designing a landscape. To divide his property into manageable areas, Drotar thought of his landscape as a series of outdoor rooms, such as the front yard above, that he could develop as time and money permitted.

At first glance, the site surrounding my little country house in upstate New York reminded me of the lost Inca civilization of Machu Picchu, an ancient Peruvian colony overgrown by the jungle. When an archaeologist hacked away at the growth years later, a stunning hillside city sprang to life. While I fantasized about a similar Indiana-Jones-style rescue of my place, developing my landscape has, in fact, required much more time and careful planning. Everywhere I looked there was work to do—the house needed repair, the land needed weeding, and landscaping was nonexistent. Though initially I was tempted to focus exclusively on projects that would produce instant results, such as repairing the house, I soon realized the value of developing a plan for the entire landscape from the beginning. Plants need time to establish themselves and reveal their beauty, and with a carefully thought-out plan, I would be less likely to make haphazard decisions I might later regret.

Inventory the site

I began by taking stock of my site. My house and 3½-acre parcel of land, located on rolling meadows outside the tranquil village of Castleton-on-Hudson, was once part of a larger 125-acre farm. Here, the Swartz family had had a booming dairy, poultry and fruit business until the late 1970s, when rising fuel costs and declining profits forced them to sell to an investor who didn't care about preserving the property. The buildings were neglected and the grass grew tall, but from the moment I looked at the small two-bedroom house, I decided that the asking price of $49,900 was a bargain. For my money I got a house that was once a barn, a new well, a dilapidated horse stable, fields of unmowed grass, a few trees and shrubs, and some incredible views.

Just a few months of walking around my land made me aware of some of its good qualities. With its gentle southerly slope, the soil warms up more quickly in the spring. Melting snow and rain freely drain down the hill without puddling in the heavy clay soil. Cold air doesn't collect, decreasing the chance of damage to hillside vegetation from untimely frosts. All this, combined with the moderate climate of the Hudson River Valley, extends the growing season and would allow me to grow plants that might not otherwise survive here.

My acreage also contained an assortment of farming implements lying in ruin amidst tall brush, tires and wood heaps. I resisted a bulldozer mentality. Someday I would resurrect the undercarriage and beams of that dying old hay wagon, rebuild it, and create a quaint roadside display. But for now it would simply rest peacefully in one of my "keep" piles. The fragments of rusted barbed wire that emerged from the ground and ambushed my lawn-mower shaft went in the "dump" piles.

"All your junk is in neat little stacks," my sister commented after seeing my place for the first time. Karen is a nun and tries to find the good in everything. Perhaps she appreciated my approach to the land.

From the beginning, I vowed to respect the land and the features prior generations had etched into it. As I developed a landscaping plan, my desire to preserve the site's rural character and work with what I had was always foremost in my mind. And by devising a plan for the entire property, rather than planting in bits and pieces, I had more opportunity to enhance what was there.

Slow and deliberate were my watchwords during the first year. I did little else on the property except haul away trash and clear weedy growth, but the time proved valuable, giving me a chance to step back and examine what I had. Through the seasons, I became aware of subtle changes that would have passed by unnoticed had I seen the site only during one time of year. I was also able to learn some of the history of the land from local people. This slow approach was a practical one as well,

1. Inventory the site

It's important to know what you have before you try to figure out what to do with it. It's easy to note buildings and other structures, large trees and bushes, the overall lay of the land. Smaller plants and finer features of the landscape require closer observation. And it's only over time that you can determine sunny and shady spots, dry and damp areas, places where snow builds up or water courses. Walk your property regularly; keep your senses sharp. Whether you make a systematic study of these things or keep track of them "in the back of your head," give yourself time to understand your site thoroughly.

2. Identify problems

Keep track of potential problems as you study your site. These may be physical—an excessively damp area, an unpleasantly windy corridor, a dying tree. Plants or structures may obscure a desired view or make it difficult to move from one place to another. Some problems are less tangible. Relationships between existing features may "feel" wrong; features you'd like to add may not seem to "fit in." Spend some time thinking about these problems—the more thoroughly you understand them, the better able you'll be to solve them.

3. Decide what you want

Some of what we ask of landscaping is functional—a place to park the car, paths to get from here to there, screening to block an unsightly view, an acceptable level of maintenance. But much of landscaping has to do with satisfying the senses, with giving us pleasure. Sometimes the things that delight us are obvious— lovely flowers, a welcoming entryway, a striking view. Sometimes it's harder to pinpoint why something is pleasurable. What you like somehow corresponds to how you feel things "ought to be." If your design is true to these feelings, and the ideas or attitudes that underly them, chances are it will be successful for you.

since I had a full-time job.

My neighbors, whose houses had once belonged to the Swartz farm and also been acquired in a state of disrepair, sometimes brought reality into my often romantic thoughts of the land. "You should get a ride-on lawn mower," my neighbor Randy advised, handing me a photo he'd snapped while I was cutting a large field with a push mower. "I call this one 'Miles to Mow Before I Sleep,'" he said.

Identify problems

Once I had a feeling for my site, I was ready to think seriously about an overall design for the property. The first step was identifying problems I wanted to solve. There were a number of them—the land was unevenly graded and access to the front of the property was inadequate, to name a few. But I felt that the problem that most needed attention in an overall design was that of scale—I had a very small house on a big piece of property. Somehow, I had to plan the features of my landscape so they weren't too big or too small for either. I knew I couldn't just plop down a modest bed of flowers in the midst of a large yard and have it look right. I wanted to preserve the sense of my site's openness without feeling as if I, or the plants, were standing unprotected in the middle of an enormous field.

Decide what you want

Looking for ideas, I immersed myself in books on landscape design. I admired pictures of large European estate landscapes, but I knew that such a dramatic look would be overkill for my tiny house. However, the books gave me an idea that really appealed to me: breaking up my site into several outdoor rooms. An outdoor room is an area of the yard with distinct boundaries that define or enclose it. The room may be private and hidden, or public and open to view. A good design allows these rooms to flow together visually as well as physically, one area enticing you into the next.

This concept seemed well suited to my property. Identify-

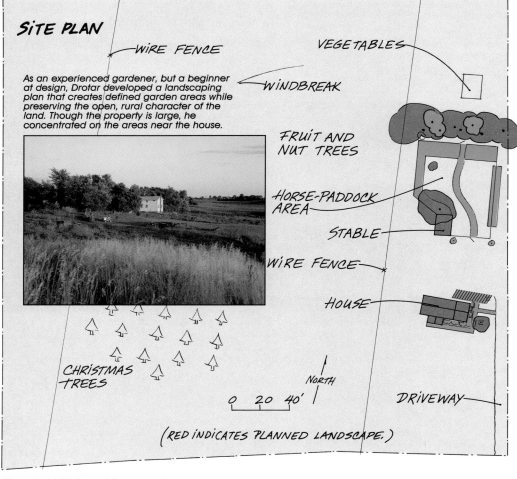

SITE PLAN

WIRE FENCE

VEGETABLES

WINDBREAK

As an experienced gardener, but a beginner at design, Drotar developed a landscaping plan that creates defined garden areas while preserving the open, rural character of the land. Though the property is large, he concentrated on the areas near the house.

FRUIT AND NUT TREES

HORSE-PADDOCK AREA

STABLE

WIRE FENCE

HOUSE

CHRISTMAS TREES

NORTH

0 20 40'

DRIVEWAY

(RED INDICATES PLANNED LANDSCAPE.)

Illustrations: Staff

An easy technique for developing a landscape design

Experimenting on paper with different landscape ideas can prevent disappointment later on. Drawing is daunting to some people, but there's an easy method for sketching out design ideas using photos and transparent overlays, as shown below. This technique works best for designing the large pieces of the landscape, such as border shapes and structures, rather than for laying out the details.

Here's how to get started. Take photos of the areas you plan to design and have 8x10 prints

made. Black-and-white prints are easiest to work with, and many photo shops can make them from negatives or slides. Shoot each area from several different viewing points; a straight-on shot is least distorted, but other perspectives can be helpful.

At an art-supply store, buy sheets of acetate, a transparent plastic, to overlay on the photos. For drawing, you can use one or more of the following: China markers, permanent felt-tipped marking pens, or crayons, in one or more colors.

Buy an all-purpose, grease-removing household cleaner, rubber-cement thinner, window cleaner or rubbing alcohol to erase your marks.

Tape a piece of acetate to the photo and start to sketch. It's easy to erase what you've drawn with the solvent and a tissue, and start again. Or draw on a new piece of acetate. You can even show the effect of adding different elements by using multiple overlays. Once you get the hang of it, have fun and see what works for you.

—Nancy Beaubaire

On an enlarged print of the color slide of Drotar's house shown below, we used a colored China marker on an acetate overlay to first outline the structures he planned to add, such as the path sketched above. Then we added other large-scale elements such as plants, filling in to show their eventual size. Sketches like this in conjunction with a plan view (right) help you get a complete picture of your design.

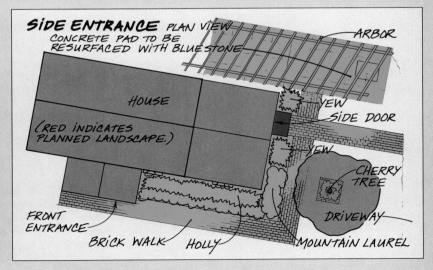

Labels on photo: WOODLAND TREES, FLOWER BORDER, ARBORVITAE, PATH, CHERRY TREES, FENCE, LAVENDER

A rebuilt stable, which is now a toolshed, marks one corner of the horse paddock. Drotar plans to further enclose this space, creating a restful country garden within. A row of young arborvitae that he's already planted on the east side will eventually screen the view of the neighbor's house. The split-rail fence, which now bounds the paddock on the north and west, will be extended around the entire perimeter of the area, leaving an entrance between the flowering cherries. With the addition of more trees, the spruced-up hedgerow will one day form a small woodland.

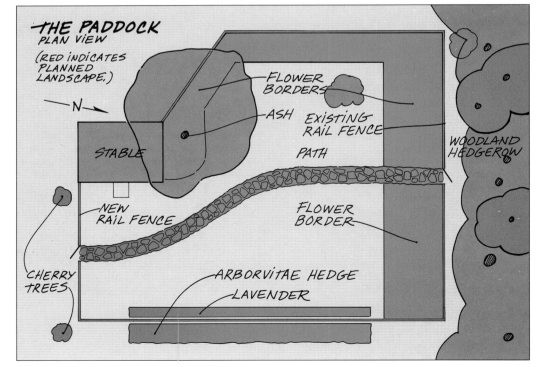

THE PADDOCK
PLAN VIEW
(RED INDICATES PLANNED LANDSCAPE.)

N

FLOWER BORDERS
ASH
EXISTING RAIL FENCE
PATH
WOODLAND HEDGEROW
STABLE
NEW RAIL FENCE
FLOWER BORDER
CHERRY TREES
ARBORVITAE HEDGE
LAVENDER

ing individual rooms would give me manageable areas of land with which to work. Within this framework, I could design smaller gardens, each with a quaint, homespun look. But as appealing as rooms were, the notion of splitting up the parcel presented an agonizing paradox. How could I successfully break the land into rooms without feeling confined or losing the overall sense of open countryside? I proceeded cautiously.

Since my property was so large, I decided to make my garden rooms on the part of the site nearest to the house, about an acre in area, where they would be most noticed and used. Existing buildings and several natural features seemed to logically divide the property into several areas: a horse paddock, which lay about 50 ft. behind the house; the rear of the house; the side entrance; and the front yard (see the site plan on p. 21). Beyond these, on the remaining 2½ acres, I planned a windbreak, a fruit and nut orchard, a planting of Christmas trees, and a vegetable garden.

Look at the big picture

Before going further with the rooms, I mentally stepped back to look once again at the whole site. I wanted to make sure I hadn't ignored any large-scale features of the property that might affect the design of the smaller areas. In fact, during the entire planning process, I found it valuable to shift my perspective back and forth between large- and small-scale features: between the whole property and the rooms, between the rooms and the plants within them. This approach allowed me to pay attention to details without getting hung up on them, and to ensure that each part of the landscape fit together to create a pleasing whole.

As I thought about it, the only large-scale problem was the wind, which howled through the windows of my house during the first winter. This prompted me to look more closely at the topography of the site. My house is situated atop a small bluff and is exposed on its western side.

Ever since I'd moved in, I had appreciated the panoramic views of the Catskill and Heldeberg mountain ranges, the Hudson River Valley and rolling fields. But it took the reality of winter to point up a problem like the wind. How could I possibly block the wind without blocking the view?

In this part of the country, the prevailing winds are from the northwest during the winter. During the summer, they shift slightly and blow more from the southwest. I realized that by planting windbreaks of fast-growing evergreens such as Austrian pine and Norway spruce to the northwest of my house, I could reduce the winter winds without blocking the summertime breezes or obscuring my view. Trees mitigate wind for a distance approximately ten times their height, so I had considerable latitude as to how far I positioned my mini-groves from the house.

Develop parts of the whole

Having solved (I hoped) the problem of the wind, I returned to the rooms. Take, for example, planning for the horse paddock and the side of the house. Both of these areas were priorities for me to tackle. The paddock was the perfect location for a quiet retreat amidst an informal English country-style flower garden. The side of the house begged to be made into a welcoming entryway.

The paddock—The boundaries of the horse paddock were quite easy to see. The entire area was sunk several feet below the level of the surrounding land. Remnants of a split-rail fence, which had once enclosed the paddock, still stretched from the shed in the southwest corner along the west and north sides. Behind the fence, an ugly hedgerow further enclosed the north side.

I wanted to preserve as much of the character of the land as possible, but were any of the existing plants and structures worth saving? My eye was drawn first to the scraggly hedgerow. Should I chop it down? Originally it had separated the paddock from a tractor road above it, but now it was a conglomeration

4. Look at the big picture

For the purposes of an overall landscape plan, it's helpful to separate the big problems from the little ones, functional requirements from "pleasure-giving" ones. Be mindful of the smaller concerns while you're looking at the big picture, but don't let them bog you down. The overall plan will guide your activities for a long time, but it should be able to change as circumstances and your ideas do. Don't make it too rigid or detailed.

5. Develop parts of the whole

Once you've sorted out the elements of the overall plan and the basic ideas it embodies, you can begin developing plans for discrete areas. The approach is the same—what do you have, what do you want, what are the problems and solutions—though the scale differs. Most important, your decisions can be informed by what you know about and plan for the rest of your property.

Set against the fence and hedgerow behind, a flower bed brightens the far side of the paddock garden. Annuals such as cosmos (background), petunias and ageratums (foreground) fill in around pink-flowered sedum and other young perennials.

of brambles, weeds and trees serving no function. Or did it? With a little effort, I imagined the hedgerow as a pleasing backdrop for this room. By adding more trees, I could enlarge it, making a woodland large enough to stroll through. This would reinforce the feeling of a haven from the outside world, and make a transition between the paddock and the rest of the property.

Once I had decided to resurrect the hedgerow, I found I could enclose the rest of the room by accentuating and adding to existing landscape features in a similar fashion. I'd reconstruct split-rail fencing around the entire perimeter, leaving an entrance on the south side, flanked by two cherry trees. The low, open fence would allow me to see a portion of the garden from the house, tempting me to come out and take a closer look.

To screen out an unpleasant view of the neighboring property to the east, I'd plant a row of American arborvitae. Inside the paddock, I've planned several flower borders surrounding a lawn. There will be a path from the entrance of this country flower garden to the woods and vegetable garden beyond. The stable now makes a perfect storage shed for my tools and mower. **The side entrance**—The side entrance (see illustrations, p. 21) is adjacent to my driveway, so

everyone uses it more often than the front door. I wanted this area to be welcoming and well surfaced, as country mud has a way of sneaking into my house. But like the other areas immediately surrounding the house, this one was a disaster, with junk trees wedged tightly against the poured-concrete basement. Reminded of my last visit to the dentist, I laboriously extracted each tree down to its roots.

Once I had cleaned up the area a bit, I could more easily see what I had to work with: a flowering cherry near the driveway, a patch of lawn, and a concrete pad surrounding an old, now-defunct well just 10 ft. from the side door. A brick path between the door and the driveway would provide easy and clean access to the side entrance, and I'll continue this path around the corner of the house to the front door. To emphasize the cherry even more, I'll fill a bed at its base with candytuft, which will bloom much of the summer. Dwarf mountain laurels planted next to the house will add seasonal color to complement yews planted on either side of the door.

I plan to resurface and extend the concrete pad, using bluestone, and to build an arbor above it, covered with wisteria and hanging baskets of cheery annuals. The stone pad and brick path will create a plazalike area, where visitors can linger and enjoy the arbor and a bubbling fountain fashioned from the old well. Protected from the summer sun by the arbor, they'll be able to gaze out toward the mountains.

Sometimes when I visit family and friends in their neat, low-maintenance suburban homes with tidy little yards, I wonder if this is all worth it. Those folks live a comfortable life. They seem to have time and money to go hiking, read literature, travel. Things I used to enjoy doing. But then I return home to the peace and beauty of the land, and I know I wouldn't trade it for all the bungalows in Bedrock. □

David Lee Drotar is a free-lance writer who gardens in Castleton-on-Hudson, NY.

Designing a Precocious Border

220 ft. of bloom in one year

by Anne Boden

I've designed residential and commercial gardens in southwestern Connecticut for eight years. I often design flower borders as part of my jobs, so it was no surprise when, in July 1986, a prospective client asked me to completely redo her 200-ft.-long flower border in an English cottage-garden style. I had seen large-scale flower borders in books and magazines, but I had never had a chance to design such an enormous perennial garden before. Delighted with the possibilities, I was confident I could use the same principles for designing this garden that I'd used for smaller ones. This approach worked just fine, even though I had to make a few adjustments as I planned the project. In this border, much larger areas of each species were required for an effect than would be needed in a smaller garden, and the border would be seen both from considerable distances and from close up, so I had to periodically shift my perspective between the two views, making sure both were attractive.

I also thought that the elegant house on the property merited a garden that appeared mature as soon as possible. The challenge of developing a plan that combined the needs of a garden as it matures over time with the client's desire for a full-looking garden in the first season was a familiar one. After investing time and money, few of us are content with a first-year garden of tiny plants and only a promise of future blooms.

Both the client and the site had exacting requirements. For the past 50 years, the existing border had been replanted with the same mixture of spring- and summer-blooming annuals and perennials—hundreds of tulips, astilbes, peonies, hostas, cleomes and impatiens. Although my client was fond of all of the existing species except the tulips, she preferred far more diversity. Her house is occupied primarily during the summer and fall, so early-spring bloomers such as tu-lips easily could be eliminated. Mauve, pink, white, blue and a touch of yellow composed her color palette, and she wanted an abundance of cut flowers and distinctive foliage textures. The existing border, viewed mainly from the house and terrace across 200 ft. of lawn, hid a lovely stone wall. Nestled so close behind the border, the wall made it impossible to enjoy the flowers from all sides. My client was eager to walk around the entire garden so she could appreciate details of the plantings. And although the border was to remain as a backdrop for the lawn, she wanted it to be more dramatic and fluid-looking than the existing rectangular border.

The site had physical problems, too. The stone wall and a row of 70-ft.-tall hemlocks behind it blocked air circulation. Under these humid conditions, fungal diseases such as botrytis disfigured the flower petals. The friable loam soil sat on a high water table, so drainage was less perfect than might be expected from the soil characteristics. Soil tests showed that in some areas the soil was too alkaline from years of annual lime applications. A lower pH, in the range of 6 to 6.5, would have been more favorable for growth of most of the perennials. The shadier parts of the garden received an average of only four hours of sun per day. The center of the garden received six hours from morning to midafternoon. While the northwest corner also had six hours of sun, it came in the early morning and late afternoon and so was of a different quality.

I began to design once I knew my client's desires and the site's characteristics. During site visits, I had videotaped the border, made thumbnail sketches and took measurements for later reference. The videotape, in particular, refreshed my memory as I worked, so I didn't need to frequently revisit the garden.

The original straight-edged border was very static. I proposed to divide it into several large beds, each with a different curved shape. The border would still look continuous when viewed from a distance, while the curves would add depth and encourage eye movement through the plantings. Positioning the beds farther in front of the stone wall would make them inviting to walk around, make more of the wall visible, and make it easier to maintain the plants and cut the flowers.

The garden seemed to divide itself naturally into three beds of varying sizes, each with its own microclimate, cultural needs and setting. One bed would be located at the sunny, southeast end of the border, placed so its boundaries wouldn't block an adjacent access gate. The wonderful grove of old hemlock trees provided a dramatic center of attention and framed an area for the middle bed. A cool environment shaded by a nearby oak tree defined the perimeter of the third bed.

I planned the shape and size of the beds with the help of a Macintosh Plus computer and two graphics programs, MacPaint and MacDraw. I drew "freehand" with MacPaint and transferred these sketches through another program, Switcher, into MacDraw, which let me fit the images in a desired scale. With this method, I could develop alternatives more quickly than I could have by drafting by hand. Once I had selected a few promising designs, I reworked the drawings by hand on graph paper until I was pleased with the shapes (drawing, facing page). As designed, the center of the garden would be a 100-ft.-long semicircular bed directly in front of the hemlocks. This bed would partially enclose a sitting area that would entice people to cross the vast lawn, relax and explore the garden. Near the gate would be a teardrop-shaped bed, 36 ft. long, and across from it an 84-ft.-long curved bed in the shady area. The beds would vary from 8 ft. to more than 20 ft. wide. Grass paths 3 ft. wide would make it easy to stroll through and care for the garden. This plan was enthusiastically accepted by my client.

Next, I turned to plant selection, a phase of design I especially enjoy. Some of the existing hostas and pink and rose peonies and astilbes could remain in the new garden, but in different locations. For new plants, I chose those with a long flowering period and interesting foliage texture, and included many suitable for

Viewed from the east, the mature-looking border winds along the edge of the lawn, framed by tall hemlocks and the stone wall. By the end of the first summer, the three separate beds appeared continuous, unified by blocks of large plants and pink and white flowers.

cutting. Plants that needed extremely dry soil were excluded because of the high water table. The existing irrigation system was modified for the new border, so moisture-loving plants could be grown. About 55 different species filled the bill, but, I must confess, once I had decided on plants that met the needs of the client and the site, my final selections were often the plants that I love.

For each plant species, I listed its height, flower color, bloom period and light requirements. (Reference books, such as *Taylor's Guide to Perennials* and *Taylor's Guide to Annuals,* and seed catalogs were helpful.) Then I categorized each according to light requirements and height, the initial criteria I'd use for placing the plants within each bed. I already knew the microclimate of each bed, so my lists of tall plants for sun and tall plants for shade, and similar lists for medium- and low-growing plants made it easier to figure out suitable locations for each species later on. I also made a color key for the flowers, so I could select plants of different colors at a glance.

Determining where to place plants is something of a juggling process. In addition to light requirements and height, I consider plant spread, rate of growth, texture, color and bloom period, all at the same time. I find it important to measure and plot out the garden on paper before planting so I can spot and avoid potential overcrowding problems in advance, as well as have a record of plant locations for later reference. For smaller gardens, I often work out the entire plan on computer, which also allows me to store designs for future use. But on this job, I found that if I displayed even one of the large beds on my computer screen, each individual plant was almost invisible. So I worked on a tissue-paper copy of the perimeter plan, outlining groupings of plants of the same species and keying them with letters for the species. Later I had blueprints made.

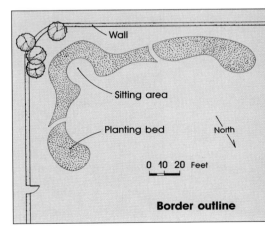

Border outline

I began with tall plants in the center of each bed: delphinium (*Delphinium elatum* Giant Pacific hybrid 'Galahad'), snakeroot (*Cimicifuga racemosa*), hollyhock (*Althaea rosea* 'Newport Pink'), peony (*Paeonia* spp.) or rose fountain grass (*Pennisetum alopecuroides*). I surrounded them with medium-height plants such as blue sage (*Salvia azurea* subsp. *Pitcheri*), phlox (*Phlox carolina* 'Miss Lin-

The feathery leaves of bleeding-heart (foreground, left) are similar to delicate meadow-rue leaves (background, left). The airy, pink flowers of both species are echoed in the adjacent cleome blossoms, and they contrast with the white flower spikes of obedient plant. Spotted-lungwort leaves edge the bed.

The swordlike foliage of a yellow daylily, cream-striped lilyturf and rose fountain grass (background, left) helps link a diverse planting in a small area. The silvery gray, fuzzy leaves of woolly lamb's-ears are a foil for surrounding green foliage. Behind the woolly lamb's-ears, annual flowers (left to right) of white and magenta sage, and pink cosmos, cleome and impatiens fill in among the perennials.

gard'), Japanese anemone (*Anemone hupehensis* 'Splendens') or foxglove (*Digitalis × mertonensis*). Sometimes I used tall plants such as meadow rue (*Thalictrum Rochebrunianum*) and snakeroot as backdrops at the rear of the bed. But I always positioned the tall plants where they wouldn't create unwanted shade. To edge the beds and ease the transition from border to lawn, I placed groups of low-growing plants such as coralbells (*Heuchera sanguinea* 'Chatterbox'), woolly lamb's-ears (*Stachys byzantina* 'Silver Carpet'), bleeding-heart (*Dicentra eximia*), Japanese star primrose (*Primula Sieboldii*), forget-me-nots (*Myosotis scorpioides* var. *semperflorens*) or lilyturf (*Liriope Muscari*).

I followed simple guidelines for harmonizing flower colors. Complementary colors have a striking effect in this garden. Clusters of yellow daylily flowers accent blue cardinal flowers (*Lobelia siphilitica*); yellow flowers of santolina (*Santolina virens*) set off blue flowering salvia. The white flower spikes of obedient plant (*Physostegia virginiana* 'Summer Snow') and snakeroot liven up pink impatiens (*Impatiens Wallerana* F1 hybrids) and spider-plant blooms. Sometimes I paired plants with two different shades of the same flower color. The pink blooms of bleeding-heart (*Dicentra spectabilis*) boldly contrast with the red flowers of coralbells, while the slightly different pinks of impatiens and cleome more subtly blend together.

When the plants aren't blooming, contrasting leaf textures, colors and shapes add interest to the border. Large, broad, dark-green, serrated peony leaves contrast with the white-striped, linear leaves of purple moor grass (*Molinia caerulea* 'Variegata'). I paired the bold, dark-green leaves of snakeroot with the fuzzy, silver foliage of woolly lamb's-ears.

I also used similarity to unify the border and to help the eye flow throughout. I grouped plants with like leaf or flower shapes but different heights, blooming period or flower color. Meadow rue and Japanese anemone are particularly effective together — the similarity of leaf shape and the overlapping bloom periods give a feeling of continuous bloom, even though the plants' flower colors are different. The delicate, blue-green foliage of meadow rue highlights the finely dissected, medium-green leaves of bleeding-heart (photo, above left). Likewise, the swordlike foliage of the grasses, lilyturf, irises (*Iris sibirica*) and hybrid daylilies (*Hemerocallis* cvs. 'Alice in Wonderland', 'Close-up', 'Ice Carnival', 'Irish Thyme' and 'Little Buckaroo') ties the garden together, despite the different flower shapes and colors of these plantings (photo, above right). I interspersed annuals — impatiens, cleome and cosmos — throughout the border. Their pink flowers bloom most of the summer, filling the gaps between the bloom times of the perennials as well as linking the various sections of the garden together visually. As the perennials fill in, I'll be able to replace many of the annuals with ferns.

I tried to unify the garden over time, as well as in space, by providing a succession of bloom in white, blue and pink. Continuous white flowers are provided by early-blooming obedient plant, followed by later blooms of gooseneck loosestrife (*Lysimachia clethroides*) and snakeroot. Iris, pincushion flower (*Scabiosa caucasica* 'David Wilkie') and blue cardinal flower furnish a succession of blue flowers. The pink blossoms of Bethlehem sage (*Pulmonaria saccharata* 'Mrs. Moon') are later echoed by the flowers of bleeding-heart; both are reinforced by the impatiens.

Grouping several plants of a single species creates visual continuity in both large and small borders. In large borders such as this one, where a 36-sq.-ft. section of the border is planted with one kind of flower, this technique has a particular impact. Color and texture combinations that may not actually be contiguous appear to blend together when seen from far away. Clusters of plants of a single species also contribute to the illusion of a mature garden.

Other "tricks" helped, too. The existing peonies, astilbes and hostas were already full-size. Some of the plants, such as meadow rue and artemisia, filled in during the first season. The fast-growing annuals covered the ground quickly. All of these effects were intensified by the quantity and size of the plants I selected. Whenever possible, I bought two- or three-year-old plants, rather than buying smaller, less mature ones or planting seeds. As a result, blocks of large, full

Repeated throughout the border, large clumps of annuals such as low-growing mounds of pink and white impatiens, and tall, pink cleome plants visually unify the border and quickly gave the garden a full, mature look. The attractive licorice-root mulch maintains soil moisture.

plants visually appeared as a solid mass, and the bare ground between plants tended to be visible only at close range.

A huge garden needs lots of plants—we used about 1200 individual plants of roughly 40 species, including seedlings started in a greenhouse on the site, purchased plants and divisions of existing plants. I didn't even consider buying plants at local retail nurseries. They usually didn't have the quantities or cultivars I needed, and even if they had, I would have wiped out their entire stock. Instead, I relied on growers of perennials who could ship me exactly what I needed. It was expensive to buy large plants—perennials in 5-qt. pots can range from $7 for an easy-to-grow species to $30 for a rare plant. My budget allowed me to purchase everything on the plan the first year. Given less latitude, I could have bought smaller plants, or started everything from seeds, cuttings or division, masking the immature look of smaller plants with lots of annuals.

Calculating the number of plants that could fit in a particular area was easy. First, I found out the usual mature size of each species from gardening catalogs and books, and then divided the total area earmarked for the species by the area required for a single plant. The result was a rough estimate of the total number of plants needed. (Bear in mind that plant growth varies depending on site and soil characteristics.) Even with these calculations, I probably ordered fewer plants than many people would. I

prefer to plant farther apart to eliminate root competition and shade, and, most important, to allow the plants to develop their form unhampered. When plants are crowded, it's difficult to appreciate their individual beauty. And maintenance is much easier if you aren't in danger of stepping on something at every turn.

Planting such a large garden presented only one new problem for me: layout. For smaller gardens, I've outlined the beds with a garden hose, or measured and indicated the edges with lime. But these methods seemed impractical here. Amato, one of the grounds crew, came up with a timesaving idea. We placed 2-ft.-high stakes every 2 ft. and connected them with white cord. After getting the approximate outline of a bed, we adjusted the stakes and cord to the exact shape.

We double-dug the beds, and amended the soil with sand, topsoil and/or peat moss where needed, which took quite a bit of time in this large garden. After planting, we mulched with fine-textured, shredded licorice root. Its gray-brown color is an attractive backdrop for the plants, and the bark reduces weeding time. This mulch also has a unique advantage—it dries out very quickly, while the soil underneath stays evenly moist.

To maintain the garden, the major chores are deadheading, weeding and staking. Minor chores include renewing the mulch, spraying fungicide, and controlling pests such as slugs, bugs, rabbits and deer. The licorice-root mulch

seemed to dissuade slugs the first year, but deer browsed many of the plants, particularly the phlox and hostas. We applied a deer repellent, Hinder, to rags tied on stakes placed near vulnerable plants. The repellent was effective if renewed periodically, but there appeared to be no deer-resistant plants in this border. I anticipate that plants in the border will need to be divided in the third summer after planting. If the garden is totally successful, there won't be any bare spots available in which to replant the divisions.

Few gardens grow exactly as planned, but this one turned out remarkably well, with only a few problems. (The existing cleome, for example, grew quite tall and looked out of proportion, but we'll replace it with a shorter cultivar.) In just 11 months from that first phone call, my client had a thriving border that looked as though it had been there forever. Of course, there will be changes. Besides substituting perennials for some of the annuals, we'll add more silver-leafed plants, such as artemisia, to the sunny bed. I've already added unusual perennial plants to the original design—bluestar (*Amsonia Tabernaemontana* var. *salicifolia*), boltonia (*Boltonia asteroides*), globe thistle (*Echinops Ritro* 'Taplow Blue') and veronica (*Veronica spicata* 'Sunny Border Blue'). All good gardens constantly evolve; that's one of the delights of gardening. □

Anne Boden is a landscape designer. She owns Forget Me Not Designs in Stamford, Connecticut.

Beds and Borders
Self-contained plantings shape the garden

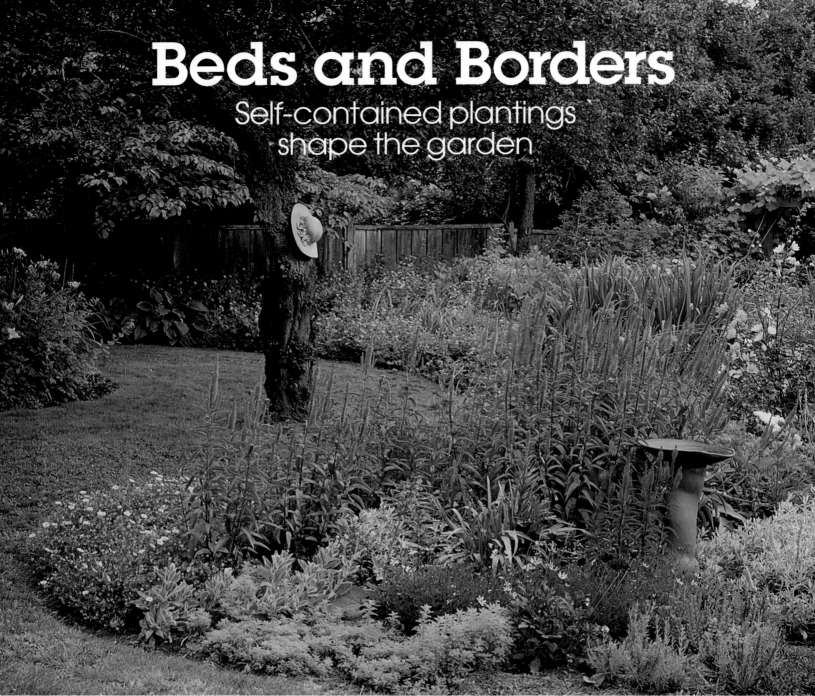

Linked by lawn, curving beds and borders organize the author's backyard into separate planting areas. A mass of purple veronicas enlivens the foreground bed. (Photo taken at A on site plan, p. 31.)

by Barbara Ashmun

One of the most versatile ways to design a garden that is rich in flowering plants and still appears unified is to divide the property into beds and borders. I'm mad about

flowers, and so are the clients of my garden-design business, but we want our gardens to look like more than collections of plants. Beds and borders help us accomplish our goal.

What are beds and borders? Island beds are free-standing planting areas that you can walk around and view from all sides. They may be round, oval, rectangular, square or irregular in shape and are usually

surrounded by lawn. Borders are generally made against a backdrop, such as a hedge, fence, wall, building or property line, and are usually viewed from only one side. Borders can have a straight or a curving edge—it usually follows the line of the backdrop.

I use beds and borders in my garden designs because they're versatile. They can help you organize your garden into distinct areas, each with a specific purpose. For example, a border of tall, screening plants will give privacy from the neighbors, while crescent-shaped beds near a patio or swimming pool can create a feeling of enclosure and intimacy. Planting in beds and borders is also a convenient way to group together plants best-suited for problem sites, such as areas with poorly drained soil or a windy exposure. Because they're self-contained, beds and borders offer flexibility in design. They can be made in different shapes and sizes and still mix well together in one garden.

Finally, beds and borders allow you to work on your garden one piece at a time. I want time to get to know a garden, understand the light, the wind, the existing trees and the shape of the land. I also need a chance to experiment, learn, improve the soil, dream, imagine and create. The day-dreaming kind of trance I put myself in to create a garden does not happen under pressure. You can develop new areas of your property in beds and borders as your time, energy and budget allow. You can create a full look and a sense of satisfaction even if other parts of the property are not complete. And you can easily re-do one bed or border without disrupting the rest of the garden.

Solving common problems

My property started with common problems—lack of privacy and unwelcome views. I bought it for its mainly sunny exposure, relatively flat terrain and ample gardening space. Although the property is 100 ft. wide and 300 ft. deep, the house sits only 40 ft. from the road. For the front yard, I wanted privacy and a nice view to enjoy from the kitchen and living room windows, as well as streetside plantings that would attract clients. In the backyard, I wanted to screen out the neighbors' yards on the south and west. I also hoped to block the view of wild areas that I wasn't ready to tackle. Beds and borders proved to be ideal building blocks for my garden. They made it easy for me to develop it slowly, but with purpose.

A border that looks two ways

The border I created along the street at the edge of my front lawn provides privacy and beauty. It's home

Sedum 'Autumn Joy' nestles beneath peach-flowered daylilies on the streetside of the author's front border. Easy-to-grow perennials, daylilies readily establish themselves in a new border or bed.

to a mixed planting of trees, shrubs, perennials, annuals and bulbs that can be enjoyed from two sides— from the house and from the street. A backbone of small trees and shrubs down the center of the border partially screens the road from my view and also blocks the house from the view of passersby. Against this backdrop, I planted drifts of perennials, bulbs and annuals on the

house side for my enjoyment and big sweeps of bright perennials along the street for onlookers.

Separating the border into two sides allowed me to work with two different color schemes. Facing the house, I planted mainly flowers in the softer hues I prefer—pale blues, pinks, purples, soft yellows, with a touch of white. Toward the road, I experimented with vibrant

In the front yard border (above), a backbone of taller shrubs and a palette of perennials provide the author with privacy and pleasure year-round. In the foreground, the red, succulent leaves of dragon's blood hug the earth in front of spiky, purple veronicas. Yellow-flowered lady's-mantle and pink hardy geraniums follow the curve of the lawn.
(Photo taken at B.)

In the "damp-garden" bed (at left), the grasslike leaves of yellow flag iris and pink flowers of geranium 'Claridge Druce' hide a cistern from view and thrive in the moist conditions. Ceramic fish made by local sculptor Katy McFadden-Benecki frolic among the iris foliage. The gently curved edge of the bed lends a flowing, graceful look to the garden and draws the eye through the plantings.
(Photo taken at C.)

oranges, reds, yellows and blues, colors to stop traffic and attract pedestrians and runners.

Although I wanted my side of the border to look interesting year-round, I began by planning the winter view from the kitchen, thinking that winter is when I most need to see cheerful colors. I started with a composition of dawn viburnum (*Viburnum × bodnantense* 'Dawn'), a shrub whose small, clove-scented, pink flowers bloom in winter, and masses of lenten rose (*Helleborus orientalis*), a low perennial whose shapely evergreen leaves are covered with delicate pink and cream-colored flowers in February and March.

To create privacy, I planted shrubs and trees, all 8 ft. to 10 ft. tall, in the center of the border. I chose a white-flowered magnolia (*Magnolia soulangeana* 'Lennei Alba') for spring color, a pink rose (*Rosa glauca*) for early summer color and red fall fruits, and a sassafras tree (*Sassafras albidum*) for its orange fall color. They don't completely screen out the road, but they do give me a feeling of separation and enclosure. And they look much more interesting than an evergreen hedge.

Lower shrubs and tall perennials enrich the picture. Facing the house, I planted spring-flowering, fragrant shrubs: pink-flowered daphnes (*Daphne burkwoodii* 'Somerset' and 'Carol Mackie'), and a Meyer's lilac (*Syringa meyeri*). I added clumps of Japanese and Siberian iris (*I. ensata* and *I. sibirica*). Closer to the front of the border, I placed pink and white summer phlox (*Phlox paniculata*), valerian (*Valeriana officinalis*), which bears white, fragrant flowers, and, to jazz things up, peonies in shades of pink and dark pink-red. Framing the border are masses of lady's-mantle (*Alchemilla mollis*), with its foamy sprays of yellow flowers, blue-flowered hardy geraniums (*Geranium himalayense*) and dusty pink-flowered sedum 'Autumn Joy'.

In late spring, the streetside of the border bursts forth with the intense colors of red-orange Oriental poppies, purple Siberian iris and fragrant, yellow-flowered lemon daylily (*Hemerocallis flava*). For summer color, I massed yellow and salmon-pink daylilies, yellow threadleaf coreopsis and blue Frikart's aster. For fall, I planted drifts of dwarf asters in shades of

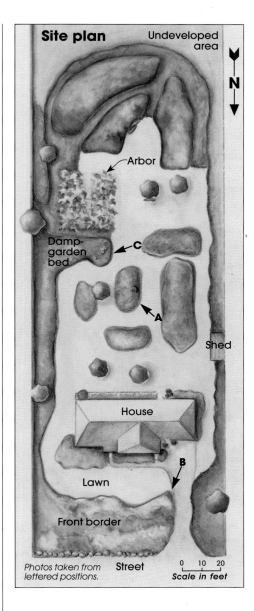

Site plan

Undeveloped area

N

Arbor

Damp-garden bed

C

A

Shed

House

B

Lawn

Front border

Street

Photos taken from lettered positions.

0 10 20
Scale in feet

blue and purple, orange montebretia (*Crocosmia × crocosmiiflora*) and red California fuchsia (*Zauschneria californica*), a low-growing sprawler. This side of the border is a wonderful four-season feature and a real people-stopper. I am so happy when I discover that the beauty I've helped to create is being enjoyed by so many others.

A bed for a wet site

My "damp-garden" bed deals with two problems: an eyesore and wet, boggy ground. The eyesore, a 7-ft. diameter cistern that the previous owner had filled with debris and topped with soil, temporarily fills with water during heavy winter rains, giving it the appearance of a small pond. My property also drains down to this area, so all the ground in front of the cistern is quite damp

as well. Turning a liability into an asset, I made the cistern a focal point for a damp garden. Within the cistern I planted irises that thrive in standing water—yellow flag iris (*Iris pseudacorus*) and the blue form of *I. virginica*. Next to the cistern, I planted blue Siberian iris and white spuria iris (*I. spuria*) along with astilbes (*Astilbe × arendsii*) in shades of pink, red and creamy white. These plants love the damp soil and flourish in this site, which is shady in the morning and quite sunny in the afternoon. In front of the Siberian iris, I grow daylilies in shades of creamy yellow and salmon-pink, and I edge the bed with lady's-mantle and hardy geraniums.

My beds and borders are small worlds within the larger garden. I developed each as the need arose. For example, my first bed covered some bare ground left in the wake of the previous owner's trailer home; the next bed united several roses that were sprinkled around the lawn. A fall delivery of irises created an emergency need for a third bed, which I hastily made by topping the lawn with 18 in. of compost and planting directly into it. (Plants in this raised bed, with its excellent drainage, have grown the most vigorously of all.)

Despite the wide assortment of plants in the individual beds, the garden holds together visually. My upper backyard, for example, is tied together by a series of round beds. Making more than one bed of a similar shape helps create a feeling of unity, as does a carpet of grass winding between them. The green grass also gives the eyes relief from flower color.

Stalwart plants for new beds and borders

I use stalwart plants, tried and true perennials that survive difficult situations without any pampering, to break new ground. I recommend you start with these plants when you make a new bed or border. They establish well, multiply quickly and are easy to move.

For heavy clay soil that stays wet in winter and spring, I rely on Siberian iris, daylilies and hardy geraniums. Siberian irises grow in strong clumps with vertical, blade-like green leaves topped by purple, blue, magenta-pink or white flowers. Plants grow from 2 ft. to 5 ft. tall,

Sunlight dances off the flowers of a hardy geranium (*Geranium endressii*), a stalwart plant for breaking new ground.

The ones I count on for ground-breaking are *G. pratense, G. himalayense, G. ibericum* and *G. endressii*. Of these, *G. pratense* is the weediest, spreading from roots and self-seeding, but it's a lot prettier than the dandelions I'd have in its place. It stands 3 ft. tall and flowers its head off in June, at the same time as the peonies and old roses. It bears an abundance of small, blue-violet flowers among deeply divided leaves. *G. ibericum*, which grows about 1½ ft. tall, has darker blue-violet flowers and works well as a ground cover. My *G. himalayense*, with its lovely blue-violet flowers, grows at the edge of the mixed border near a drift of lady's-mantle. The flowers are similar in color to those of *G. ibericum*, but the leaves are more daintily divided. *G. endressii* has bright pink flowers that are almost too intense, and it blooms from summer through autumn. From tiny divisions I took in spring, it spread into a substantial ground cover the first season and flowered all summer. I wish I had thought to plant 'A.T. Johnson' instead, a cultivar with lighter, creamier pink flowers, but oh well....

For dry shade, two of my favorite perennials are Mrs. Robb's spurge (*Euphorbia robbiae*) and bishop's hat (*Epimedium* spp.). The dark green, glossy, evergreen leaves of the spurge form rosettes at ground level. In the spring, flowering stems bearing bright yellow flowers shoot up about 2 ft. tall. The plants spread quickly by underground runners, but you can easily keep them in check by digging out the extras. Be careful to wear gloves when you touch spurge because the milky juice inside the stems can irritate your skin and eyes.

Bishop's hat has many species. Most are evergreen, and all are tolerant of dry situations. Delightful plants for the shade, they bear medium-green, heart-shaped leaves and early spring flowers in shades of yellow, white or pink, depending on the species. My favorite (so far) is *E.* × *rubrum*, a pink-flowered species. Blooming about the same time as early daffodils, it makes a lovely ground cover beneath flowering crabapples, plums or cherries. □

and expand to 3 ft. across by their third year in the garden. Some of my favorites are deep purple 'Caesar's Brother', vibrant pink-red 'Eric the Red', and burgundy 'Chilled Wine'. The irises are striking when they bloom in early summer and restful afterwards, when their foliage serves as a good backdrop for later-blooming flowers. These deep-rooted plants tolerate sun or part shade, and standing water.

Daylilies are also clump-forming perennials; they have grassy, outwardly arching leaves, and flowers in shades of yellow, orange, peach, pink, red, lavender or white. It's hard to choose from the abundant offerings. The blooms are big, but last only one day. The spent flowers look like rumpled socks or crumpled crepe paper, so it's important to pick them off frequently or plant the daylilies where they will be viewed only from a distance. In my front border, these plants have come through six winters of standing water and full sun with flying colors. They have also survived elsewhere in my garden in partial shade and in dry places.

Hardy geraniums range from small ground covers to large border specimens. They'll grow in sun or partial shade, in dry or wet soil. And they are beautiful, besides. [For a profile of hardy geraniums, see *Fine Gardening*, # 29, pp. 32-35.]

Barbara Ashmun is a landscape designer and teaches gardening classes in Portland, Oregon.

Gardening With Miss Jekyll
Her principles still work today

by Andrew Ducsik

Many people call Miss Gertrude Jekyll (1843-1932) the greatest artist in horticulture and garden planting who ever lived. In the early 1900s, she and architect Edwin Lutyens designed dozens of gardens for English country houses. When I first learned about Jekyll and Lutyens' work, I realized that the gardens they created were so expensive and labor-intensive that they would be

Author Ducsik lives in an old neighborhood filled with mature forest trees. Half his property is woods; the rest is divided by walls, fences and hedges into a series of garden "rooms" (above).

impractical today. But pictures of the gardens looked very, very beautiful, and caught my interest.

Jekyll wrote several books on gardening, and I have read and reread them many times over the years, slowly digesting her ideas. I've found that those ideas still speak to us in 1989, and that it's possible to adapt them to small, private gardens. Three general principles stand out as most significant to me: grouping

colors to harmonize or contrast, choosing foliage for year-round textural interest, and seeking the gardening style most appropriate for a particular site. I try to incorporate these principles into my own garden and into the gardens I design. (For more on Jekyll, see p. 36.)

I live in Chestnut Hill, an old, traditional neighborhood in the far northwestern corner of Philadelphia, separated from the city by the woods of the Wissahickon Valley. My house is a small cottage, set back 350 ft. from the road, with woods on three sides. My land covers about half an acre, and is roughly 400 ft. long by 70 ft. wide. I've left more

COLOR COMBINATIONS

My "bold" border mixes the bright reds and yellows of daylily and geranium flowers with the strong yellows of variegated aucuba foliage (top). Plants with silver or gray foliage make an attractive counterpoint to plain green leaves or to the brighter colors of flowers (above left). The "hot" orange daylily blossoms contrast with the "cool" violet rose-of-Sharon (above right).

than half the property as woods, the way it was originally, and developed it simply by adding ferns and wildflowers. Walls and hedges divide the rest of the land into "rooms" with carefully planned plantings inspired by Jekyll's principles.

Color combinations

Color was very important to Jekyll. She thought that the warm colors of the spectrum (reds, oranges, deep yellow) were best grouped together in harmonies or gradations. The cool colors (blue, violet, pale yellow) were most striking if grouped in contrast—thus she combined blue with white or very pale yellow. Jekyll also believed that the warm colors and cool colors enhanced each other as the eye became saturated with one and craved the other. Green could be used to

moderate other colors and to tone down an entire composition. White and silver-leaved plants could serve a like purpose.

These color principles were worked out and best shown at Munstead Wood, Jekyll's own garden, in a border 200 ft. long and 14 ft. deep, backed against an 11-ft.-tall sandstone wall. It was a mixed border, with small trees and climbers planted against the wall, and shrubs, annuals, perennials and bulbs throughout, designed to bloom from early July through September. Both flowers and foliage contributed to the color pattern. The border began with cool blues or mauves at the ends, and ran through graduated harmonies or contrasts of color to a "hot" center of reds and oranges, all blended with greens, silvers and whites at the right places.

I could never plant or maintain a 200-ft. border in my garden, but one of the great wonders of Jekyll's work is that pieces of it often are as beautiful as the whole. Any section, because of the color rules, works as well in isolation as it does in the full border. Thus, in a small garden, you can develop a border limited to one part of the spectrum, maybe focusing on the splendor of the warm and hot colors, or, for a spot where the light is less intense, going for a cool border of blue, white and pale yellow. Another approach, this time straight Jekyll, would be to have a border of special color, as she called it. She suggested gray, gold, green or blue as possibilities, but she was smart enough not to make these gardens or borders of one color only. She knew that the beauty of any color is often heightened when

THE ROLE OF FOLIAGE

Foliage color and texture are important in a garden. Evergreen hollies form a backdrop for the bright flowers of chrysanthemums and New England asters (top). Hostas 'August Moon' and 'Frances Williams' add color in the summer (above left). The foliage of barberry 'Crimson Tide', holly 'Cajun Gold', winged beech and sensitive fern provides color and texture all year (above right).

seen in conjunction with an opposite or contrasting color, and she frequently placed touches of white and yellow to lend dash to her green border, or deep orange as a counterpoint to blue.

I've tried this approach in my garden with some success, and made a "bold" border of bright and dusky reds and bright yellows, toned down with cream, pale yellow and lots of green. This border has two peaks of bloom. The first is in May, when the deep red—almost black—rhododendron blooms. The second occurs in late June and continues through July, with daylilies in bright red and all shades of yellow. Groupings of red geraniums give color all season.

But the border doesn't rely just on flowers for color. Colored foliage sustains the interest from April to September.

Evergreen aucubas splashed with yellow, variegated hostas and variegated euonymus give the needed bright yellows. The dusky reds are provided by 'Bloodgood' Japanese maples and 'Ruby Glow' barberry. Ferns and white-variegated conifers add light-green and cream foliage, respectively. I've recently put in a clump of variegated grass to supply more cream foliage, and planted some *Heuchera* 'Palace Purple' to strengthen the dusky-red foliage accents.

The role of foliage

Jekyll knew that foliage also supplies ingredients of texture and form that flowers do not. What's more, foliage is less ephemeral: if evergreen, it's with us for the whole year, and if deciduous, for more than half the year. In her own border, she

used yuccas, with their spiky evergreen profile, as full-stop punctuation marks at both ends, and bergenias, with their fleshy rounded leaves, as edgings. The woolliness of gray and silver foliage was a perfect accompaniment for blue, pink or white flowers, and the black-green needles of yew set off brighter flowers. Of course, in Jekyll's woodland gardens, the greens were all-important. Ferns and other foliage plants helped in the transition from garden to woodland and then served as a frame for her "flowery incidents"—patches of woodland flowers such as trilliums, lilies-of-the-valley or foxgloves, set in glades or nooks in her woods.

I've tried to follow Jekyll's lead and be much more aware of how foliage effects can enhance my flower gardening. I use Christmas, ostrich, interrupted and

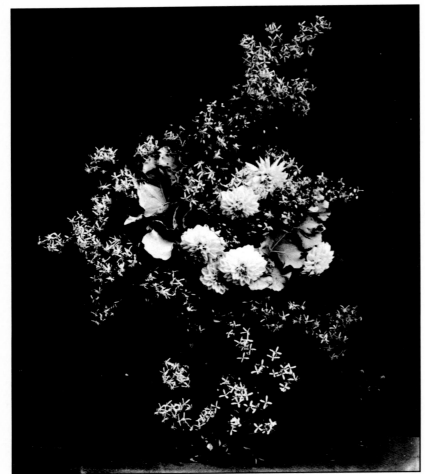

Jekyll took up photography in 1885, and kept a series of personal photograph albums. She repeatedly photographed her own garden at Munstead Wood, and also took pictures of plants, homes, objects and people. This photo, which Jekyll took in 1906, illustrates her many talents: she gathered the white dahlias, Clematis Flammula, sea kale and magnolia leaves from her garden at Munstead Wood, and arranged them in this glass "Munstead" vase that she had specially designed. A collection of her photos and accompanying text is presented in Gertrude Jekyll: A Vision of Garden and Wood, *by Judith B. Tankard and Michael R. Van Valkenburgh (Harry N. Abrams, Inc., 100 Fifth Ave., New York, NY 10011; 1989; $38.00 postpaid).*

THE JEKYLL REVIVAL

Gertrude Jekyll is remembered both for the gardens she designed and for the books and articles she wrote. Born into an intellectual, upper-class English family, Jekyll spent the first half of her long life pursuing all things artistic and beautiful. She was skilled at painting, embroidery, fine metal and wood work, and flower arranging, as well as gardening, and practiced all of these at Munstead Wood, her home in Surrey, England. She developed a style of life, a style of homemaking, that emphasized simplicity, quality, naturalness and beauty.

At about mid-life, Jekyll teamed up with a young architect, Sir Edwin Lutyens, and together they designed dozens of gardens for country houses. Some of these gardens are considered among the finest ever made. The books she wrote during this period are based on her observations of plants in these gardens and her own garden. After World War I, tastes changed, however. Work designing country houses and gardens dried up, and Jekyll's books went out of print.

In 1981, Jekyll's books began to be reissued, and they found a new audience of readers. Appreciation for the work of Jekyll and Lutyens seems almost unbounded these days. Numerous authors have expressed admiration for their work. Decayed gardens of the partnership are being restored, and new gardens inspired by their style are being made.

To learn more about Jekyll's work, I'd recommend two of my favorite books. Jekyll's own *Color Schemes for the Flower Garden* (Salem House Publishers, Topsfield, Massachusetts, 1983) is a practical guide to color theory and how to apply it in your garden. She recommends plant combinations, and presents detailed planting diagrams that manifest her ideas. Jane Brown's *Gardens of a Golden Afternoon* (Penguin Books, New York, 1986) describes the work of Jekyll and Lutyens, and gives a thorough tour of their gardens, putting these into historical perspective, and interpreting how the ideas can be applied today. —A.D.

cinnamon ferns to tone down a too-hot color combination. I use the glaucous-leaved hostas, such as *Hosta Sieboldiana* 'Elegans', in a border with a blue theme; in the woodland to cover dying daffodil leaves; and to define pathways. The bright yellow of the hostas 'August Moon' and 'Frances Williams' have also served me well in the hot or "bold" border, giving almost six months of color and form.

In another area, I've used evergreen hollies as a background for a border of autumn flowers. The hollies add a bright dash and give year-round interest. Some are green, and many are variegated varieties. Some have leaves edged with cream or gold, and some are blotched with these colors. I enjoy looking at them in deep winter, and they cheer me as much as Jekyll's hollies must have cheered her as she walked through her garden in winter, admiring how they contrasted with the white-birch tree trunks.

Appropriateness

What may have been Jekyll's most vital contribution, her most lasting legacy, was her general attitude toward life and her striving for quality and integrity. This was reflected in her own garden and home. In her book *Home and Garden,* she cried, "O! for a little simple truth and honesty in building, as in all else that is present to the eye and touches daily life." Jekyll was genuine, as were her knowledge and taste. This meant that she didn't need to be loud or showy. Her principle was restraint and the striving for beauty in everything.

"Is it right?" and "Does it fit?" were the questions she always asked. In her garden, she sought what was most appropriate for each area. Thus, her flower border was a glorious sight of full color—nothing timid here. It was carefully thought out, the interweaving drifts blending beautifully into one another, with just the right gradations of colors. In her woodland, she sought "a green thought in a green shade," a feeling of secrecy and seclusion. Her spring garden must have been crystalline in color, a concentration of freshness. And finally, her secret garden was just that—it was hard to find the entrance or exit. No gaudy canna lilies there, but a dark background of ferns and Solomon's-seal and old-fashioned flowers such as woodland phlox.

I'm seeking a similar feeling of integrity in my own gardening, but after practicing in four gardens (two belonging to my family and two of my own), I realized that I needed to better manage my resources. I've learned not to attempt too much in terms of quantity, and instead to aim for a high degree of finish and quality. Thus, I intensively cultivate only part of my half-acre property. Maintaining the rest of the property as woodland is less fussy and

Photo: From *Gertrude Jekyll: A Vision of Garden and Wood,* Sagapress, 1989.

APPROPRIATENESS

The woods that extend from my house to the street call for a casual, natural style of gardening. All I've done in this area is remove the lower tree limbs, plant some ferns and wildflowers, and install a few garden ornaments.

less labor-intensive. This frees me to refine and polish my special borders and to keep my handkerchief-size lawn in perfect shape. By concentrating most of my energy on this relatively small area, I have the time to work toward a very elusive perfection.

I'm also mindful of Jekyll's principle of appropriateness. My town is three centuries old and very traditional. Here, the English ideal of flower borders, boxwood hedges, and conventional garden ornaments such as sundials and classical statuary seems most appropriate. It might be equally suitable for New England, areas of the South, and the Pacific Northwest. In Florida, the Mountain States and California, more contemporary styles, newer materials and a different selection of plants could be effectively used and

would not seem incongruous.

Exercising restraint is another challenge for me. For a long time I've wanted a traditional Lutyens' teak bench for my garden terrace. They're sold in two sizes. To me, the scaled-down 6-ft. bench doesn't have the same graceful proportions that the original has. The problem is that no matter how beautiful the 8-ft. original, it would completely dwarf my small terrace. It would look ridiculous, and not be appropriate, so I've settled for a 6-ft. Adirondack bench.

Similarly, I regret that my garden has no water feature. I'd love to have a small reflecting pool or a spouting mask, but I fear that the addition of even one more structure to my very small garden would be just enough to push it over the edge and take away the all-important feeling

of restfulness and peace. I'm determined that if a pool or fountain is to appear, something else must go.

A final word about Gertrude Jekyll. The most significant aspect of her philosophy is its agelessness. It worked in 1900, and it works today. It worked in England and it works in Los Angeles as well as in Chicago or Connecticut. What's of value is not the specifics. Jekyll's principles of appropriateness, restraint and integrity are timeless and open to all of us. We may have limited resources and scope, or a restricted garden space, but these same ideas are still as valid as when they were set out by Jekyll almost 100 years ago. □

Andrew Ducsik designs and maintains gardens in Chestnut Hill, Pennsylvania.

Nature as Inspiration

Learning to use what we see: Jens Jensen and the Prairie School of landscape design

by Robert E. Grese

As a landscape architect with a longtime interest in native plants, I am both delighted and concerned with the recent interest in gardening with wildflowers. I love to see people appreciating plants that form an important part of our natural heritage. I am concerned because the current vogue for wildflowers has not changed the attitudes of most gardeners and designers, who often use native species simply as substitutes for horticultural varieties. For too long, many gardeners have emphasized the exotic and rare, preferred showy contrast to subtle harmony, and suppressed, rather than worked with, natural plant systems and cycles. We need instead to look to native plant communities not just for plants but also for patterns and processes that can serve as the basis for landscape designs.

Many of us share a fascination with spontaneity in the landscape, with things that seem beyond our planning and control. Note the favorite places that recur in our memories of childhood: the space under a protective tree canopy, a winding stream or creek (not yet channeled in concrete), a woodlot with a variety of undergrowth and wildflowers, or an undeveloped wetland at the edge of town. These have in common the qualities of surprise, diversity and mystery that are often lacking in designed landscapes. The challenge is to incorporate these same qualities into the places where we live and work.

Over the past couple of years, I've been examining the work of turn-of-the-century landscape architects and gardeners who used native plants in their designs. I'm finding a rich but largely forgotten heritage that has much to offer those of us today who are interested in designing with native plants.

Nowhere was the interest in landscaping with native plants stronger than in Chicago. In the late 19th century, when Chicago architects such as Louis Sullivan and Frank Lloyd Wright were declaring their independence from East Coast traditions in architecture, Jens Jensen, Ossian Cole Simonds and other Chicago landscape architects developed a language of design for the prairie states of the Midwest. They didn't apologize for the lack of hills; rather, they celebrated the horizontal. Instead of lamenting the difficulties of growing delicate varieties, they championed the common roadside plants then thought to be weeds. With designs that instilled an appreciation of natural cycles and beauty, they sought to redress the alienation of urban people from nature. Their gardens and parks were meant to acquaint people with the indigenous beauties and to inspire the preservation of what wild nature remained.

Jens Jensen was a dominant figure in the Chicago "school" of landscape design. A Danish immigrant, whose first job in Chicago was as a streetsweeper, Jensen built hundreds of public parks and private gardens throughout the Midwest.

(For more on Jensen's life, see the sidebar below.) His designs were inspired by the regional landscape. He insisted, however, that they were not mere copies of nature but idealizations that highlighted certain aspects or features of the natural landscape. Colors, textures, sunlight and shadow, seasonal change, and the careful manipulation of space were his means of evoking deep emotional responses like those we feel in the natural landscape.

Jensen was a keen observer of plants in the wild. He felt that certain species had ecological and aesthetic "personalities." Oaks, for example, were a symbol of constancy; hawthorns a symbol of the prairie. His designs reflected his understanding of the character of native plant communities. He noted that a handful of species usually dominates a stand. For instance, in native grasslands, two or three grass species may comprise 80% to 90% of the total, giving the stand a unified look through the seasons and over the years. The arrangement of plants within a given plant community is also distinctive. In a closely spaced maple woodland with its closed canopy, trees grow straight and tall as they compete for precious sunlight. The result is a pattern of vertical trunks. In contrast, the open growth of undisturbed oak woodlands creates a pattern of heavy and irregular branching. (See the photos on pp. 40-41 for examples of the ideas discussed in this article.)

When adapting design ideas from native plant communities, Jensen used the same dominant plants and arrangements, adding other plants for accent or contrast. Accordingly, he made mass plantings, unlike many of his contemporaries, who favored specimen plants. Where a plant name appears on one of his plans, it usually meant six to 15 plants rather than one or two. Jensen avoided the then-current practice of planting in rows and geometric configurations even in "naturalistic" compositions. He instructed that some plants be placed very close together with others more distant, as might be found in the wild. In one planting of trees, for example, he specified spacing "all the way from three to four feet apart to ten to fifteen feet apart." Jensen also repeated plants throughout a design, much as an Impressionist painter used dabs of one color in differing amounts across a canvas to help unify a composition. The same type of patterning occurs in nature where one species is clumped in a part of the woods or meadow, with occasional specimens dotting the boundary or distant view.

The manipulation of space is a difficult but powerful aspect of design. We tend to be object-oriented, so it often takes time to become comfortable thinking of plants, rocks and landforms not just as shapes and volumes but as boundaries or modulators of space. The outdoor environment can be thought of as a series of rooms. The character of these rooms often depends on their size, shape, soil conditions and exposure, and the plants in and around them. The high arching branches and open understory of a floodplain forest create a majestic, cathedral-like room. Much of our park design seems to be based on this model, with high-branched trees and grassy understory. In contrast, an oak woodland with an understory of small trees and shrubs has much smaller,

more intimate rooms. Open environments such as prairies or mountain meadows are large rooms with adjacent landforms and the sky as boundaries.

Jensen carefully articulated space in his designs. He often worked at a grand scale for estates and parks, but he was equally adept at handling small sites—sometimes less than an acre. By making the edges of meadows irregular and punctuating the central, open areas with islands of vegetation, he ensured that the whole was never visible from any one perspective. He set smaller outdoor rooms at the edges of larger open spaces to provide views into and across the main space. When these intimate rooms were open to the sky, Jensen called them "clearings" or "sun openings" because of their contrast with the dark forest bordering them.

Like a painter, Jensen was particularly adept at working with natural light. He placed "sun openings" carefully to create an intriguing pattern of light and shadow that changed throughout the day. Jensen felt very strongly that people ought to have contact with the cycles of nature. He provided paths and gathering places where people could watch the sun rise and set or observe the changing patterns of light on the broad landscape as clouds drifted across the sky. Jensen was also intrigued by the warm hues of the low-angled sun of autumn evenings, and he often placed plants such as sumac, sugar maple, goldenrod and aster where the sun would inflame their foliage or set their feathery seed heads aglow.

We too can use sunlight as an aesthetic tool. With careful attention to the direction and angle of the sun during different

A Jensen biography

Jens Jensen was born in 1860 in Slesvig, Denmark, where he gained an early appreciation of nature from the lanes and fencerows of his father's farm. He attended a folk high school that emphasized Danish cultural traditions and the celebration of nature and its seasons. At Tune Agricultural School, he studied botany, chemistry and soil science in preparation for a life as a farmer. In 1884, soon after graduating, he emigrated to America with his fiancée, Anne Marie Hansen.

After short stints at farming in Florida and Iowa, Jensen landed in Chicago and went to work as a common laborer in the West Parks. In 1892, he became foreman over many of the West Parks, but in 1900, he was fired for refusing to participate in the political graft then rampant in the Chicago park system.

Jensen then began to design the landscapes of private estates and summer homes for the Chicago elite, experimenting in his designs and relying increasingly on native flora he had observed on the outskirts of Chicago. Earlier in

Jens Jensen stands on the site of Lincoln Memorial Garden in Springfield, Illinois (facing page; photo taken c. 1935).

the 1890s, he had struck up a friendship with Dr. Henry Cowles, pioneer ecologist and botanist at the University of Chicago, and together they studied plant communities. Gradually, Jensen incorporated the patterns they had observed in the wild into his design work. He had become a member of the Special Park Commission in 1899, and for several years surveyed lands around metropolitan Chicago for a system of preserves where examples of the region's finest wild lands would be safeguarded.

In 1905, a new commissioner hired Jensen as general superintendent and landscape architect for the entire West Parks system. Jensen redesigned Garfield, Douglas and Humboldt Parks, as well as many smaller parks and playgrounds. In Columbus Park, he started from scratch, creating an idealized midwestern landscape.

Jensen's reputation and private commissions continued to grow. He collaborated with Louis Sullivan, Frank Lloyd Wright and many other architects of the "prairie school." Other practitioners of the period combined elements of many landscape styles, but Jensen emphasized the unique qualities of each site. He restricted formal geometry to vegetable gardens and small spaces surrounded by

"wild" nature. His insistence on nature as the inspiration for design made him less than popular with many of his colleagues, but they respected his ability to evoke strong emotional responses with his landscapes.

Jensen was an active conservationist. He helped to organize the Prairie Club, which led "Saturday walks" to acquaint city people with the wilds around Chicago. He organized The Friends of Our Native Landscape to promote a love for natural places and to fight for their protection. With the help of these organizations, Jensen laid the groundwork for many of Illinois's state parks and fought for the preservation of the Indiana Dunes as well as for the establishment of a prairie national park.

In 1935, at the age of 75, Jensen moved to Ellison Bay, Wisconsin, where he founded The Clearing, which he liked to call a "school of the soil." Here students learned landscape architecture as well as other arts and crafts, based on the direct observation and celebration of nature and cultural tradition. He wrote about his philosophy in his book, *Siftings*, published in 1939 and now out of print. Jensen continued to design and work on conservation projects until his death in 1951. —R.E.G.

In a natural plant community, a few species usually dominate a stand. Here, on the slopes of Mt. Rogers in Virginia, mountain ash and a few red spruce are scattered throughout a cascade of rhododendrons.

The unplanned arrangement of sedges in this wetland in The Dolly Sods Wilderness Area in West Virginia is pleasingly rhythmic without being regular.

A note on the photos

The photographs accompanying this essay were selected to show how design principles and ideas can be derived from nature. It's easier to see how some of these scenes inspire designs for public parks or large estates, where the scale is large, rather than designs for smaller, residential landscapes. But the relationships shown can also work at small scale. Imagine, for example, that the rhododendrons at left are a massed planting of knee-high wildflowers, or that the islands of vegetation in the picture at bottom right on the facing page are knee-high, waist-high or head-high shrubs. Like Jensen, be aware that you can evoke nature in the garden without having to copy it.

times of the day as well as at different times of the year, we can make the landscape not only more interesting but also more comfortable. To get a sense of how "sun openings" work, look for them in a natural woodland. You'll see marked differences in the effects of the light depending on whether the light is behind, to the side of or in front of what you're looking at. Backlighting, for example, can create interesting silhouettes and vivid shades of green as the sun highlights translucent leaves. Plants with thin, dull leaves such as sugar maple or witch hazel are particularly striking when backlit. Plants with thick, shiny, glossy leaves such as rhododendrons are more effective when lit from the front or side; the reflection can brighten a dark understory.

Jensen incorporated few garden structures in his designs. They were too intrusive, too much evidence of "the hand of man." The exception was the circular stone seats that he called "council rings." Here's how Jensen described these rings:

"I often bring into my compositions a council ring built of stone, of a diameter of nineteen to twenty feet and with a fireplace in the center, with an elevation of eight to ten inches above the ground. The idea of the ring is partly Indian and partly old Nordic, though the construction is modern. Practically, the ring brings people close together, and the fire chases away the mosquitoes....From a spiritual standpoint, there is something within us that loves the fire, and gathering about it has a social leveling effect that puts us all on a par with one another. A council fire gathering is the most democratic institution we have. We are, after all, children of the primitive, and we like to go back to it."

These rings served as the social centers of Jensen's gardens, the settings for conversation, storytelling, drama and music. Where they survive, such as in Lincoln Memorial Garden in Springfield, Illinois, people still gather in them to enjoy the out-of-doors.

In his later work, Jensen was particu-

Photos, pp. 40-41: Robert E. Grese

Backlighting can create striking patterns in a landscape, as shown in this scene from the Great Smoky Mountains.

This outdoor room occurs at the edge of an oak wood in Waterloo, Michigan. Open to the sky, the room is screened around its perimeter by the dense woodland undergrowth.

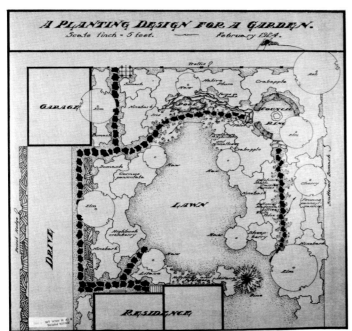

In this prototypal plan for a small site, Jensen included an outdoor room, a council ring, and massed plantings of native shrubs, trees and flowers.

Islands of vegetation divide this wetland on Assateague Island, off the coast of Maryland, into smaller areas, creating interest in the observer in what lies beyond the various boundaries.

larly aware of designing with time—not just daily changes and seasonal variation but the transformation of a landscape over decades, even centuries. He frequently sought to connect his designs with the history of a site, preserving or restoring bits of the historical landscape. He also sought to connect to its future by making celebrations of these restorations. For instance, in 1936, he enlisted groups of Girl Scouts and Boy Scouts to plant white-oak acorns on the hillock surrounding the council ring at Lincoln Memorial. Today, many of this group still sense an ownership of the grove of trees that stands there now.

I am currently exploring ways to continue public involvement in native plant-ings. Last summer, a group of fifth graders from a local school in Ann Arbor, Michigan, helped me plant a prairie meadow in a local children's park. In my mind, there is a value in people experiencing the beginning and intermediate stages in creating a landscape so that they can more fully appreciate the mature stages in later years. An instantly green landscape seems less precious and more expendable.

Jens Jensen's principles and design ideas are as pertinent now as when he first used them. As in Jensen's day, we need more gardens, parks, office parks and roadsides where people can become reacquainted with the native flora. When working with native plants in our gardens and other landscapes, we must look to nature for our inspiration and recognize our plantings as part of a larger system. If we only substitute native plants for exotics in conventional plans, we've accomplished very little. We must concentrate instead on cultivating our ability to read, understand and adapt the patterns and forms we see in the natural landscape. I think we can strive for new criteria for evaluating landscape designs and gardens, criteria that include regional and ecological appropriateness. □

Robert Grese is an assistant professor of landscape architecture at the University of Michigan School of Natural Resources.

Illustration: Courtesy of Art and Architecture Library, University of Michigan

Designing with Nature

A landscape architect and a gardener team up

An entryway bed of native plants recreates a dry prairie close to home. The garden's naturalistic design was a collaboration between Judith Stark (right), a landscape architect, and homeowner Hattie Purtell (left), an accomplished gardener and trained botanist.

by Judith Stark

When Hattie Purtell set out to express her love for Wisconsin's gentle landscape, she hoped to grow native plants on much of her property—five acres of woods, fields and river bottom—in a garden design that would reflect natural habitats. But after several years, Hattie realized that her training as a botanist and her many years of gardening hadn't prepared her to design a garden that corresponded to native ecosystems and also pleased her eye.

Hattie came to me for help. Like many other accomplished gardeners who hit an impasse over design, she was frustrated. Although we were friends, she hesitated to call. She had several concerns. Could she afford a landscape architect? Would my design incorporate her ideas or ignore them? Could we work together comfortably? She took stock of our friendship, my interest in design inspired by nature, and the time and money she'd already spent, and she decided my services would be a good investment.

I followed my usual planning process. First, Hattie and I walked around the site as she outlined her vision of the project and described the local climate. I encouraged her to write down everything she wanted from her property. By combining her "wish list" and my suggestions, we put together what landscape architects call a program, a guide for developing the design. Since Hattie wanted to retain many features of the existing landscape, our program called for fine-tuning rather than starting anew.

First steps

We set five overall goals. First, we wanted to distinguish habitats—areas with different growing conditions—and plant them with suitable natives, while evoking the spirit of the Wisconsin landscape. In effect, we would create small plant communities. Second, we planned to make general refinements throughout the property, such as creating views and adding garden accessories. Third, we would add plantings with fall and winter interest that could be viewed from indoors. In areas of year-round high visibility, we planned to emphasize plant form, leaf shape and texture rather than flowers. Fourth, we intended to highlight views of the river and to incorporate it into the design. Finally, Hattie hoped to avoid watering, spraying or fertilizing the native plants, so we had to choose them carefully.

With these guidelines in mind, we were ready to start the design. Hattie's property runs along the Milwaukee River and is surrounded on three sides by beech and maple forest. The house nestles against the forest on the north end of an old farm field. We identified six different habitats: dry prairie, mesic (moisture-balanced) prairie, mesic woodland, wet woodland, woodland edge and riverine (river edge). We were delighted to think of the enormous variety of plants we could grow.

From inside the house, the forest presented a blank wall of greenery. We realized immediately that we could not improve the beauty of the woods,

Shade-loving perennials—among them, ferns and trilliums—intermingle in the shade of pale-trunked aspen trees, while white-flowered sweet cicely fills in the foreground.

The contrasting forms, textures and leaf colors of plants in the entryway prairie provide year-round interest. Nestled below a backdrop of purple-flowered spiderwort, the drooping leaves of prairie dropseed make a striking contrast to the silver-leaved pussy-toes bordering the bed.

which are underlaid by massive drifts of spring ephemerals, plants that virtually vanish after they bloom. But we could open the woods for views and paths. We cleared enough brush and trees so one could sit on the terrace, in the kitchen or in the master bedroom and watch the river splash over rocks just 100 yds. away. We also opened views to especially interesting trees, such as a majestic beech or a multi-trunked basswood. These framed spaces lend a sense of depth to the forest. One of my gardening friends describes them as "fingers into the woods."

It took a lot of persuading to convince Hattie to remove trees, and I still think she should remove more. Perhaps in the winter, when the river looks the most dramatic, with its black water channeling through the white, snow-covered ice, she will relent. We all cringe at the prospect of cutting down trees, yet I believe good views justify some thinning.

Along the river, we developed paths that twine among the vistas. At strategic spots, we placed wooden benches as invitations to linger. We cleared spaces along the riverbank to accentuate large boulders where visitors might perch and watch the lulling motion of the current. A secluded plateau along the river will soon be developed into a secret picnic spot. We've also found a perfect place for a shoreline water garden.

Designing with native plants

Closer to the house, the habitats required more detailed plans. First, I developed a base map that included dimensions, slope, drainage, existing vegetation and sun and wind patterns. Hattie and I had a good time working together. While I drew the base map, she put together a list of her favorite native plants, noting characteristics such as plant height, bloom time and leaf color. Fortunately, I had seen all of these plants in their natural habitats and had grown many myself, so reviewing the lists was easy. It's important for a designer to be very familiar with the plants she selects, especially traits such as invasiveness or changes in appearance throughout the growing season.

Next, I drew a planting plan. Emulating plant arrangements I'd often observed in nature, I sketched irregular areas, mostly diamond-shaped, edge to edge. Within these shapes, I arranged masses or drifts of the same species, since they create a greater impact than a few plants dotted about. I composed neighboring masses and drifts so they contrasted strongly in form, in height, in leaf shape and in texture. I also strove for harmonious or dramatic combinations of color and considered time of bloom.

We planted two different habitats flanking the stone walk that leads to the south entrance of the house. In a hot, dry open area, we made a mini prairie, and in the shade of a large maple tree, we made a mesic woodland. The soft-gray, weathered siding and blue-green shutters of the house provide the ideal color background for the silver, gray, blue-green or dull green leaves of the prairie plants.

In the prairie, we massed 11 to 30 plants of each species. About ⅓ are grasses and the rest are forbs (mostly deep-rooted perennials or self-seeding annuals adapted to low moisture and nutrient-poor soil.) The slender leaves of native grasses such as side-oats grama (Bouteloua curtipendula) and prairie dropseed (Sporobolus heterolepsis) make an airy contrast to the yucca-like foliage of rattlesnake-master (Eryngium yuccifolium) and the coarse, hairy leaves of purple coneflower (Echinacea purpurea). The prairie bed is edged with heuchera (Heuchera sp.), with its round, green leaves, and pussy-toes (Antennaria sp.), with its narrow, silver leaves. We also included favorites such as flowering spurge, butterfly weed and asters. As part of Hattie's ecological approach, we leave the flower heads and seed stalks intact as forage for birds and animals, creating an attractive fall and winter garden.

For the shady woodland, we chose species that flourish in the southern Wisconsin mesic forest. We avoided spring ephemerals and plants that might not maintain a fresh look throughout the growing season. As we had in the dry prairie, we planted in drifts, but here our color palette was shades of rich green, ranging from the wide, shiny leaves of wild ginger to the delicate leaves of lady fern and Solomon's seal.

In a grove of aspen trees near the back door, we planted more woodland natives, including ferns and trilliums, two of our favorites. We interwove them in groups and have been delighted with the lacy interplay of shapes and textures. Our selection focused on royal, lady, wood and maidenhair ferns, which we knew would not be too invasive.

A sunny spot in the lawn offered the ideal location for a mesic prairie. Here we planted grasses and forbs in a curved island bed to break up the lawn area and contrast with its smooth, mown texture. We positioned taller plants, such as queen of the prairie (Filipendula rubra), yellow coneflower (Ratibida pinnata) and rough blazing-star (Liatris aspera) in the center and stepped down to shorter plants like little bluestem and blue-eyed grass (Sisyrinchium campestre).

Our efforts to establish a wet woodland edge have not proved entirely satisfactory. Much of what we planted proved too low-growing or insignificant to be appreciated from the terrace near the house. Deer devoured the Turkscap lily and others of our favorite wetland plants. We're still hoping to find satisfactory herbaceous plants for this area and to place woody species with special fall and winter interest close to the house.

Sometimes it's hard to find the native plants we'd like to grow. It is our policy not to dig from the wild unless the site has been committed to development, in which case we form a rescue committee with our friends and relocate as many native plants as possible before the bulldozers move in. For the most part, however, we obtain plants from small nurseries that propagate natives, or propagate them ourselves. Producing a rare plant from seed is one of gardening's greatest thrills.

Finishing touches

For the final touch, we chose decorative objects and structures that match the garden's informal spirit and can be left outdoors all year, giving us something to look at during the long Wisconsin winter. A wooden arbor, fashioned by our contractor from unstripped cedar logs, marks a path between the mesic prairie and Hattie's vegetable garden across the road. A wood slab bench encircles a large tree in the forest and other rough-hewn wood seats are dotted around the property. Birdbaths, chiseled from local limestone, provide an invitation for birds.

After working together on the garden for three or four years, Hattie and I are even better friends. Throughout the process, we maintained close contact, which is crucial for a truly successful design. We've enjoyed each step of developing the design and are delighted with our accomplishments. Now we are eagerly looking forward to collaborating on future projects. □

Judith Stark is a landscape architect in the Milwaukee, Wisconsin, area.

An arbor of cedar poles, covered with a climbing rose, marks the passage between a prairie planting and a vegetable garden.

A plant-rimmed tidal pool on the rocky coast of Maine (left) might have been the model for the garden pool below, designed by Kurt Bluemel. Drawing inspiration from nature's loveliest scenes is a fundamental principle of Japanese garden design.

Japanese Ideas for American Gardens

Five principles of design to use at home

by Claire Sawyers

When people learn that I once worked as a gardener for a Japanese landscaping company, they usually ask if I have a Japanese garden. Though I helped maintain the famous temple garden of Tenryu-ji, in Kyoto, Japan, as well as lovely residential gardens, I would not try to duplicate their features here. To my eye, pagoda lanterns and stone wash basins look out of place in American gardens. I admire the way Japanese gardens reflect the culture, history, resources and natural landscapes of their native land, and I think American gardens should do the same. Happily, many of the design principles that make Japanese gardens so appealing also work in America. Here are five principles of design from Japan that I hope will inspire you to make your garden more rewarding—and more American.

Capture the essence of nature
In classical Japanese gardens, Mother Nature is the model, and the gardener strives to distill nature into its most beautiful moments. Japan is

a chain of steep, largely-wooded volcanic islands. Rocks, trees and water dominate the natural landscape, so Japanese gardeners place the same elements in artful arrangement. Rocks are carefully "planted" to resemble natural outcroppings. Water is coaxed into tranquil ponds and channeled to resemble mountain streams. Trees are planted at angles to look as though wind and erosion played a role in their growth.

To capture the essence of nature in your garden, study the plants and natural features that distinguish your area and property, and comprise their "genius of place." It's jarring to see a property amid majestic deciduous woods that is landscaped with dwarf conifers, or a house in the West sitting on a patch of verdant lawn amidst straw-dry hills. If you live in the Pine Barrens of New Jersey, celebrate the pine woods and bogs in your garden. When you build a pool, model it on the ponds, tidal pools, marshes or streams of your area, not the blue waters of the Caribbean. Recognize that problems— a wet corner of the yard, or hot summers—are opportunities to bring bog plants and heat-tolerant ornamentals into your garden.

Another way to capture nature is to allow her to run free. Until recently, Americans have been pioneers, wrestling with wilderness. Now, with little wilderness left, many of us welcome a bit of the wild into our backyards. You can do this by permitting plants to naturalize, and leaving some accidents—if you accept nature as a master gardener, you will find interest and beauty in the tangled branches of a fallen tree. Pause before you fetch the chain saw. Decay and death are part of life, and the bleached skeleton of a tree can add drama to the garden. When you see dwarf crested irises growing on "nurse logs" in the forest, you learn that death is inseparable from life and rebirth.

Develop beauty from function

Garden features should serve a purpose, or appear to do so. In Japanese gardens, what we call "ornaments"—stone lanterns, wash basins, fences, gates, bridges, stepping stones—originally served some purpose. Stone lanterns, for example, lit the grounds for evening activities. Today, in modern Japanese gardens, stones may be stacked to suggest abstract lanterns, but their location still follows tradition, and so they retain some integrity. Walls and

fences have followed the same kind of evolution. In ancient Japan, they protected property from livestock and wildlife. In modern Japan, they are largely ornamental, but retain their traditional designs.

American gardeners can draw on their own heritage to find garden features with purpose and beauty. Originally built to mark boundaries and protect property, American fences have evolved into many regional styles—the zig-zag split rail fences of Virginia, the fieldstone walls of New England, the adobe walls of the Southwest. Look at the traditional fences in your area for inspiration. Rather than import Japanese wash basins, American gardeners might consider the familiar cast-iron hand pump. Styles vary

A winding path leads through the branches of a fallen but still-living cherry tree in a Connecticut garden. Appreciating accidents of nature is part of Japanese gardening.

across the country just as with fences. Place the water pump where it will look as if it's used—not in the front yard, not smothered with perennials. You have to create the illusion of usefulness to make the pump, or any feature, a convincing part of the garden.

Scale is also vital for ornaments. Miniaturizing destroys their sense of purpose. Munchkin-sized wishing wells, windmills and barns, to my eye, make a mockery of our rural landscapes.

Treat everything in the garden as an opportunity to add to its beauty. If you're installing a water spigot, make it an ornament, too. Your clothesline, barbeque grill,

doghouse, tool shed, garage, swingset and sandbox, driveway, swimming pool, and mailbox can all double as garden ornaments if you use care when you design, place and plant them.

Use materials at hand

In Japanese gardens, the paths, fences and other features are usually made of native materials and recycled items. Even in the gardens of the wealthy, the materials are humble. Old roof tiles chinked with clay become garden walls; foundation stones become wash basins; old bridge footings become shoring for ponds. When new materials are used, they are natural or only subtly altered, so they blend with the garden. Bamboo culms (stems) form fences, and paths are laid with gravel.

The principle is to build with what's at hand. The celebrated English gardener Gertrude Jekyll put it this way in 1900: "I always think it is a pity to use in any one place the distinctive methods of another. Every part of the country has its own traditional ways, and if these have in the course of many centuries become 'crystallized' into any particular form we may be sure that there is some good reason for it and it follows that the attempt to use the ways and methods of some distant place is sure to give the impression as of something uncomfortably exotic, of geographical confusion, of the perhaps right thing in the wrong place." Using Japanese roof tiles in America tends to give the opposite

effect from the simple elegance the Japanese strive for. Seeing a wash basin made of a Japanese building stone here only makes me wonder about the shipping bill.

Strive to use indigenous materials in your garden. Plain logs of durable native woods such as eastern red cedar, black locust or osage-orange, should be to American gardens what bamboo is to Japanese gardens. Made into steps, benches, lamp posts, trellises, fences and rustic gazebos, they connect the garden to the landscape around it. Why import teak benches when America has a colorful tradition of shaping willow and birch into rustic furniture? Paths of mulch, gravel, crushed oyster shell, stone or corn cobs reflect regional traditions.

Recycle materials when you build your garden. A friend of mine recalls how residents of Muscatine, Iowa, used buttons to pave paths and driveways. The buttons, discarded from a local factory, were made from freshwater oysters fished from the Mississippi River. In city gardens, recycled cobblestones and brick seem especially appropriate for paths and patios.

Marry the inside to the outside

In Japan, houses and gardens blend together. Most of the famous Japanese gardens and their associated villas or temples seem inseparable; one cannot exist without the other. Sliding doors open to the outside and allow the garden to be enjoyed from the inside. Open air verandas connecting rooms are more

Garden features look suited to their region when they use local materials and traditional designs, as shown above by the tableau of naturalized daffodils, a wall of native fieldstone and a barn-red building, and, below, by the white fence and gate.

like covered walkways than hallways. Buildings on stilts over ponds or streams allow you to observe the water more closely than when you're in the garden. Natural building materials harmonize with the land.

American gardeners can marry their homes and gardens too. A premier American example is the house known as Manitoga, designed and built by Russel Wright, an industrial designer who retired to Garrison, New York, to demonstrate how man could live in harmony with nature.

He built his house on a cliff overlooking an abandoned quarry, which he turned into a pond. Boulders form the floor, stairs and even some of the furniture of the house, and a tree trunk serves as a central support post. The views to the pond below connect inside and outside.

Even if you'll never build your own house, let alone a Manitoga, you can strengthen the bond between your house and garden by treating every window and doorway as a precious connection between indoors and outdoors. Arrange your furniture to take advantage of the views, and design the plantings to draw your eye outside. Create privacy not by drawing the curtains, but by planting around the perimeter of your property. Views that change with the seasons are more rewarding than dusty blinds.

If you don't have a porch, deck, or patio, add one or all. They provide comforts of the house, yet pull you outside. And compared to adding a

conventional room, they are affordable. Leave planting pockets between the stones of your patio, so it can bloom like the garden.

Involve the visitor

Japanese gardens involve the visitor. For example, in gardens meant for strolling, the stepping stones are spaced to break your stride, or a streamlet spills over the path, so you have to cross open water. You are subtly forced to notice the garden. The more you touch, smell, hear and

notice in the garden, the more magical the effect.

Many of the methods used in Japanese gardens to involve visitors can be adapted readily to American gardens. For instance, reward strollers with a path that offers a series of sights. Avoid open spaces sporadically punctuated with beds or ornaments; visitors will feel little urge to move through a garden without starting and ending points. And a path that disappears from view piques our curiosity. We want to find out what's at the end. We're pulled into the garden. Even with small, urban lots, a simple path leading around the house can provide distinct garden views.

Thoughtful recycling brightens two American gardens. Leading over a bridge made of recycled curbstones (above), the path invites visitors to explore the distant streamside and garden. The circular foundation of a silo becomes a lily pond in a Pennsylvania garden (right). Recycling is a characteristic of Japanese garden design.

Create your own design

The lessons of gardens that catch your eye, whether they're Japanese, English, German, French or American, lie in the principles of their design. Whenever you see a successful garden, strive to understand its distinctive qualities, and then adapt them to your site.

We're a young nation with a magnificent natural heritage. We've often echoed gardens from older cultures, like a child who parrots a parent without knowing what the words mean. I think we can study the timeless principles of design that make great gardens, and use them to celebrate our great American landscape. □

Claire Sawyers is the director of Scott Arboretum, on the campus of Swarthmore College, in Pennsylvania.

A wall of windows looks out on a woodland garden in fall, bringing the outdoors inside.

A gravel path in the author's garden wends past pink- and white-flowering rhododendrons and curves out of sight around an evergreen holly. Effective paths draw visitors into the garden and call attention to its most attractive features.

Paths to Beauty

Four design principles will lead you in style

by Joe Parks

Why do you enjoy visiting some gardens more than others? The secret often lies underfoot. In the most alluring gardens, the paths that you tread—whether they're made of bricks, stones, grass or mulch—have been carefully laid out to lead you through the garden and reveal its beauty.

Paths are one of the most important elements in a garden. First and foremost, they're a practical necessity for getting around the garden and for guiding visitors through it. But paths also provide a framework—a skeleton, if you like—that links the elements of a garden together, making the total more than the sum of its parts. And paths affect the way you view a garden; a well-designed path creates anticipation for what lies ahead and focuses attention on the garden's best features.

You don't have to be a landscape architect to design an effective path. I'm an amateur gardener with no special training—just 50 years of experience. After considerable study, much trial and many errors, I've found that a few basic principles make a path both practical and artful.

Create mystery with curves

A path that curves is inviting. A straight path, particularly in a small garden, leaves little to the imagination; if we can see everything all at once, we feel less inclined to move through a garden. But a winding path obscures the distant view and thus piques our curiosity. We wonder what we might find around the bend. Even if your path has only one gentle curve, your visitors will feel encouraged to investigate and enjoy the pleasure of guessing what comes next.

A path of stepping stones surrounded by moss meanders over a dry stream bed in a woodland garden. The stones appear to have been arranged by nature, belying their careful placement by the author.

Billowing plantings along a pine-needle path vary the width of the passage. On all garden paths, visitors tend to pause in wide sections and to keep moving in narrow sections.

Trailing perennials planted along the edge of a cut-stone path soften its sharp edges, an appropriate touch for an informal garden.

The uniform curve, neat edges and smooth surface of a brick path combine to make an inviting, formal approach to the front door at its end.

You need to conceal from the eye what lies beyond a curve. Sometimes the terrain will help; sometimes existing trees or shrubs will provide a reason for a curve. Usually, though, you'll have to arrange plantings to block the view. I use evergreen shrubs such as rhododendrons and hollies to make my curves blind.

Lead with pleasures

Around a curve, offer something to attract the eye and entice the viewer to take a closer look. A glimpse of a flower bed or a bench draws visitors along a path and rewards their journey. My garden path winds in and out through my large collection of rhododendrons. To avoid monotony, I planted many small beds of perennials and small trees and shrubs along

the path, each designed to provide a special attraction at some time during the year—a mass of primulas or gentians, a bed of astilbes, a witch hazel.

Give your path a destination: a place to sit, a special view, or just a loop that leads back—few of us like to find we've arrived at a dead end.

Invite pauses

It's one thing to get visitors to start down a path but another to get them to pause and enjoy what surrounds them. Here's where subtlety in path design comes into play. Like pools of water along a rushing stream, occasional wider sections in a path encourage people to slow their pace. On the other hand, straight, narrow sections in a path encourage visitors to keep moving. Simply by controlling the

width of a path, you can modulate the mood of your garden from energetic to restful.

You can also use steps to slow people down and to increase variety along the path. My garden has very little slope, but I've built steps where I want visitors to look around.

For two people to walk abreast comfortably, a path should be at least 4 ft. wide; for people to walk single file it should be 2 ft. wide. Steps should be at least 4 ft. wide, for safety and to allow plants to trail over the edges.

Use an appropriate material

The materials you use for your paths also have an effect on how visitors view your garden. A straight brick walk and a meandering moss path create entirely different impressions.

Photos: lower right, Susan Kahn; facing page, Mark Kane

There is a variety of materials that can be used to build paths. Concrete, brick, stone, concrete pavers, gravel, mulch, grass, dirt, moss—alone or in combination—all make fine paths. In deciding what to use, consider the mood you wish to create as well as cost, installation and maintenance.

Because of their straight, uncompromising lines, concrete, brick, concrete pavers and cut stone paths are best suited to a formal garden. But you can integrate them into an informal garden by curving the path and varying its width so that it looks more like a country lane. It also helps to plant trailing plants along the edge of the path to soften the hard lines.

Properly installed, bricks, concrete pavers and cut stones require little maintenance and are easy to walk on. But they are relatively expensive to buy and require skill to install.

In a natural-looking, informal setting, choose materials that recall paths found in nature, such as moss, gravel or mulch. The mood they create is restful and casual; they invite the visitor to enjoy the garden at leisure.

Materials for informal paths tend to be much less expensive to purchase and are more easily installed than materials for formal paths. Choose grass, moss or dirt, and I promise you'll get plenty of "oohs" and "ahs"—but you'll also have plenty of maintenance. Grass must be mowed and weeded. It grows poorly in shade. Worst of all, it won't stay put; you'll have to keep it carefully edged or in a trice you'll have grass popping up among your choice perennials. Moss tolerates shade and requires no mowing, but it hates foot traffic and needs constant weeding. Dirt is the most natural of all path materials, but even when earth is carefully pounded down, rain (or irrigation water) quickly turns it soft or muddy. It also serves as an open invitation to grass and weeds.

In my experience, the best choices for an informal path are natural stone, gravel or mulch. One of the most elegant informal paths you can have is natural stepping stones surrounded by moss. Stepping stones should be as large as you can easily handle; stones less than 12 in. across in any direction soon become unstable and make for uncomfortable walking.

I particularly like gravel paths. They are easy to make, need little maintenance and, once packed down, are easy to walk on. I use ¼ in. or ⅜ in. bank-run, washed gravel for my paths. Larger gravel is difficult to walk on. Gravel paths should be at least 2½ ft. wide because plants along the edge inevitably spread into them.

Mulches such as bark, wood chips and pine needles make unobtrusive, dry paths. But mulches are slow to pack down and become walkable, they break down quickly and they tend to have poorly defined edges that require marking, lest feet wander off course.

Whatever material you choose, remember that a path is more than a means of getting around without stepping on plants. With a little forethought, you can design paths that will make it a pleasure to visit your garden. ■

Joe Parks has built more than ¼ mile of paths through his six-acre garden in Dover, New Hampshire.

Flowering annuals and perennials along a winding grass path pull the viewer forward in anticipation of the pleasures to come.

A Crowd of Perennials

Tightly packed plants provide eight months of show

by Nancy Carney

I've learned over the years that I can enjoy a rich succession of flowers and foliage from March until November by spacing perennials together much closer than the books recommend. In the oldest gardens on my property, dozens of species grow 1 in. to 2 in. apart. The trick is growing the right mix—plants that occupy the same space at different seasons, or tolerate crowding and shade. My gardens include early spring bloomers that die back as taller plants overtop them, ground covers that abide months of growing in the shade of taller neighbors, and late-maturing plants that come up through the crowd and then burst into bloom. As one species wanes, another flowers, and all persist year after year with very little care from me.

I'm going to focus on one of my plots, a dry shade garden, but keep in mind that much of what I say applies to other conditions. I have crowded gardens in full sun and crowded gardens in wet spots, too. The chart on p. 56 gives plant lists for shade, sun and wet gardens, and the drawing on p. 57 gives my spacings for the main plant groups I use. I chose plants for the chart that are easy to grow and long-blooming and that have foliage that stays attractive. Think of them as suggestions for getting started. I'll mention many other plants in passing as I go on. When your new garden takes off, add new plants, starting with those that have proved themselves in your own location. If you're not sure what to try, ask a local nurseryman. You're bound to succeed: I've grown at least a hundred different species under closely spaced conditions, and I'm sure there are still more that will work.

I'm not going to talk in depth about design, but it's important. What's the point of growing lots of plants if they don't look good together? When I start a new garden, I think about color combinations, fragrance, flower and foliage shapes, plant heights, cultivation, and time of bloom. If you're a novice gardener, don't let this list scare you. Think about design, but remember, it's *your* garden. If you like a particular plant, color, fragrance or leaf shape, then emphasize it. Please yourself.

I take my time when I design a new garden, but I know from the start that nothing is final. I draw up a list of suitable perennials and pencil them in on graph paper, or simply walk around the plot and place pebbles and sticks where I want plants. After viewing the markers from the house and various locations on the property for a few weeks, I plant. As my tastes change, or nature changes the backdrop, I adjust. I have gardens that started out pink or white and are now yellow and orange. I often move plants in

In April, narcissus and daffodils in bloom stand above shade-tolerant ground covers in author Carney's willow-tree garden (above). The white flowers are bloodroot (*Sanguinara canadensis*), and the violet flowers are anemones (*Anemone blanda*). A forsythia hedge blooms in the background. In midsummer (left), new plants flower above a mat of shade-tolerant ground covers that includes lungwort, ginger and bloodroot. On the right are the spotted flowers of auratum lilies, on the left is the aurelian lily 'Pink Perfection', and throughout are hostas, daylilies and astilbes.

bloom, watering every day until they're settled in again. Spring transplanting might be easier, but I like to see the flowering effect immediately.

Crowding in the shade

Dry shade is supposed to be a problem condition, but I've had no trouble crowding perennials on a site that should be as tough as they come: The garden is under huge weeping willow trees, with willow roots everywhere. The soil dries out completely during summer droughts, but in early spring it has standing water.

The earliest plants to emerge and flower are small bulbs, mainly snowdrops, daffodils and narcissus. I marvel that the snowdrops bloom in March while the ground is still as hard as a block of ice. The small early bulbs persist indefinitely. You may find their longevity hard to believe, but you wouldn't if you could see me trying to work a shovel into a clump of snowdrops, 'February Gold' daffodils and ferns at the base of one willow. This combination gets thicker every year.

The shortest perennials, bulbs aside, include lungwort, periwinkle, rue anemones, wood phlox, violets, wild ginger, foamflower and sweet woodruff. All are very tough and tolerate the combined shade of trees and, later, taller perennials. In the fall, when the taller plants die back, the shorter perennials become visible again, so I want plants with exceptionally good foliage for fall as well as spring. I allow

the low perennials to spread through the bulbs and taller perennials. In my experience, they do not choke out anything else.

Among the shortest perennials, however, there are many species that will spread vigorously unless checked—lily-of-the-valley, Jacob's-ladder, bloodroot, common primrose, barrenwort and lamium, among others. I've planted them throughout the willow-tree garden, but not with the well-behaved plants I've already mentioned. Instead, I combine them with each other, or with some of the taller perennials, such as daylilies, hostas and ferns.

After the show of spring bulbs, the weeping-willow garden takes on the look of a perennial border, full of foliage and flowers. By the end of May, peonies, irises and Oriental poppies open on the partially sunny edges. Toward the shadier center, Jack-in-the-pulpits, bleeding-heart and Virginia bluebells are ending as trilliums, wild geraniums, violets, foxgloves, Japanese irises and sweet rocket blossom.

By early summer, a new group of plants appears. Garden loosestrife, daylilies, astilbes, phlox, hostas and lythrum reach full size and prepare to flower. Except for the garden loosestrife, the summer species have many varieties. With proper selection, you can have flowers of each species for most of the summer season. My first daylily blooms in early May and my last, 'Autumn Prince', in October. Catalogs and nurserymen will help you create a succession of your own favorite species.

By midsummer, bulb lilies are exuberantly sending their flower stalks up right through other plants, and one lily or another keeps blooming through fall. Asters, bugbane and Japanese anemones also flower in the fall, and as the summer plants wane, the foliage of the shorter spring-blooming perennials reappears and Jack-in-the-pulpits show off their scarlet seed cones atop foot-high stalks.

You may have noticed that many of these plants are wildflowers, or garden standbys. Long ago it occurred to me that wild plants are beautiful, free, and more likely to survive in a crowded system than tame cultivars are. I collect wild plants (except those that are rare, endangered or intolerant of transplanting) on my own property and in the neighborhood. I also collect the garden plants that persist around the foundations of abandoned farmhouses, on the theory that they're survivors. Keep an eye on the roadsides and fields in your own locality, get permission, and bring the plants you like into your garden. Watch out, though, for invasive species. One fall I brought woodland sunflowers (*Helianthus strumosus*) into a perennial bed. They took over, and were ineradicable. In the end, I dug out most of the other perennials and smothered the sunflowers with layers of newspaper and mulch. The next spring, my bulbs came up through the newspaper but the sunflowers didn't, and I replanted the perennials I'd saved. I still love the woodland

	SPRING	SUMMER	FALL
S H A D E	**Lungwort (Pulmonaria spp.)**—Several varieties. Oval leaves with metallic spots; flowers that turn from pink to blue. 5 in. tall. Excellent ground cover. **Bloodroot (Sanguinara canadensis)**—Huge, rounded leaves through spring and summer; daisylike white flowers. 8 in. tall. A native. Self-seeds and spreads rapidly. **Ferns**—Many varieties, including maidenhair (Adiantum spp.), Goldie's (Dryopteris Goldiana), royal (Osmunda regalis), Christmas (Polystichum acrostichoides) and Japanese painted (Athyrium niponicum var. pictum). 1 ft. to 4 ft. tall. Lovely foliage plants.	**Hostas (Hosta spp.)**—Many varieties. Huge rosettes of oval leaves in many textures and colors; white to lavender bell-like flowers, some fragrant. 6 in. to 4 ft. tall. **Daylilies (Hemerocallis spp.)**—Many varieties. Flower colors may be less vivid on shaded plants. **Balloon flowers (Platycodon grandiflorus)**—Small oval leaves; white, pink or blue single and double flowers on wands. 2 ft. to 3 ft. tall. Buds look like balloons.	**Jack-in-the-pulpits (Arisaema triphyllum)**—Huge leaves on 2-ft. stems; hooded flowers in spring and clusters of red berries on stalks in fall. 2 ft. tall. A native. **Bugbane (Cimicifuga spp.)**—Several varieties. Ferny foliage; white, airy, wandlike flower clusters. 3 ft. to 5 ft. tall. Nice vertical accent. **Anemones (Anemone japonica)**—Several varieties. Large lobed leaves; white to red single or double flowers from August on. 1 ft. to 3 ft. tall. A choice fall-flowering plant.
S U N	**Daylilies (Hemerocallis spp.)**—Early-blooming varieties. 6 in. to 4 ft. tall. **Oriental poppies (Papaver orientale)**—Hairy lobed leaves; huge white, pink, red or orange flowers. 3 ft. tall. Dies back in summer. **Peonies (Paeonia spp.)**—Many varieties. Deeply lobed, leathery foliage; white to red single and double flowers. 1 ft. to 4 ft. tall.	**Heliopsis (Heliopsis spp.)**—Many varieties. Nondescript foliage; daisylike yellow to orange flowers for months. 4 ft. tall. Among the longest-flowering perennials. **Phlox (Phlox paniculata)**—Nondescript foliage; fragrant white to purple flowers until frost. 3 ft. tall. Visited by hummingbirds. **Coneflowers (Rudbeckia spp.)**—Several varieties. Nondescript foliage; daisylike pink or white flowers with brown metallic centers. 2 ft. to 3 ft. tall. A native.	**Blue mist shrub (Caryopteris × clandonensis)**—Gray-green delicate foliage; blue misty flowers from August on. 3 ft. tall. **Asters (Aster spp.)**—Many varieties. Nondescript foliage; daisylike flowers in white, yellow, blue, pink, red and purple. 6 in. to 5 ft. tall. Some are natives. **Hardy chrysanthemums (Chrysanthemum spp.)**—Many varieties. Much-branched compact plants with daisylike flowers from white to red. 1 ft. to 3 ft. tall. A good cultivar is C. × rubellum 'Clara Curtis'.
W E T S O I L	**Virginia bluebells (Mertensia virginica)**—Oval leaves die back in summer; flowers start pink and turn blue, on graceful stalks. 1 ft. tall. **Common primroses (Primula vulgaris)**—Crinkled, straplike foliage; pale-yellow flowers. 8 in. tall. **Iris Kaempferi and I. Pseudacorus**—Lance-shaped, blue-green leaves; huge flat flowers. 3 ft. tall.	**Astilbes (Astilbe spp.)**—Many varieties. Ferny, leathery foliage; flowers in plumes of white, pink, lavender and red. 6 in. to 5 ft. tall. **Purple loosestrife (Lythrum Salicaria)**—Several varieties. Nondescript foliage; wandlike flower clusters in pink to purple. 3 ft. to 4 ft. tall. Invasive. **Daylilies (Hemerocallis spp.)**—Many varieties. Fountains of lance-shaped leaves; lily flowers in a range from yellow to purple. 6 in. to 5 ft. tall. Indispensable.	**Hibiscus (Hibiscus spp.)**—Several varieties. Huge heart-shaped leaves; plate-size single flowers from white to red. 4 ft. to 6 ft. tall. **Ferns**—Many varieties. Attractive foliage. 1 ft. to 4 ft. tall.

PICK A PACK OF PERENNIALS

Author Carney, with anguish, has winnowed her list of species that thrive in crowded gardens and picked a few to get you started. There are three groups—for shade, sun or wet soil—with the plants listed in order of flowering or their most attractive season. Carney chose plants that are easy to grow and long-blooming and that have foliage that stays attractive a long time.

sunflower, but now it grows alone and lavishly beside a stone fence among rampant maple-roots.

Getting started

I start new gardens whenever I have time, but I'll talk about starting in the fall. I plant bulbs first. I space them as I want to see them in March, April or early May: daffodils and narcissus 1 ft. apart, snowdrops 6 in. apart (they eventually self-seed and mat together). I give no thought to where the later perennials will go, because they emerge readily through the spring bulb foliage. Usually I set the larger bulbs deeper than recommended so that I'm less liable to hit them with a shovel as I set perennials later. I plant the smaller bulbs with a knife in shallow holes. Within a year, all have moved up or down and reached the depth they like. In my garden, the bulbs of snowdrops and star-of-Bethlehem are often at the soil surface. I leave them. They sought this depth, and they'll have leaf mulch for winter protection.

I space other perennials largely by height—closer for short plants, farther apart for tall ones. I place the spring-blooming ground covers at a spacing of 3 in. to 6 in. between plants—for example, a lungwort 3 in. from a violet. But it's backbreaking work at the 3-in. spacing, so for the last decade I've leaned toward plants that spread rapidly and positioned them 6 in. apart. I put the taller, summer-blooming plants 1 ft. apart—a phlox, say, 1 ft. from a daylily. For each species, I set plants 3 ft. to 5 ft. apart, depending on my supply and how much I want of that species' color, fragrance and foliage. One type of daylily, for instance, would be 3 ft. to 5 ft. from a daylily plant of another kind.

I sometimes put two plants in the same planting hole. I often grow tall lilies like the 6-ft. aurelian hybrids with another perennial at their base, such as a hosta or a daylily, because the rodents seem less apt to eat them then. Some of my lilies have been thriving in such crowded states for ten years. I also plant colchicums along the edges of my gardens in the same holes with spring ground covers. The colchicums show off their beautiful foliage in the spring, and when the leaves die back, the

summer perennials hide them. Then in the fall, as most of the garden withers, the colchicums send up their crocuslike flowers.

It's impossible to keep track of all the plants in a crowded garden, so I occasionally slice into a bulb or a root ball when I'm dividing or moving plants. I've never worried about it. I simply reset the pieces and count on the plant to regenerate. A more conscientious gardener might tag everything with markers, but I can't stand to see something unnatural in my gardens. Sometimes I'll place a small rock or stick atop the mulch to flag a plant I want to remember, but generally I let the plants fend for themselves.

Care

I find that crowded gardens require much less work than plantings spaced by the book do. I keep my gardens mulched year-round, largely because mulch is a convenient way to provide the enrichment crowded plantings demand. Plants that survive crowding will grow up through thicker layers of mulch better than less stalwart species will. During the mowing season, I spread 2 in. of grass clippings over the gardens. In the fall, I bag leaves from my lawn (and sometimes from my neighbors' yards) and spread them on the gardens 4 in. to 6 in. thick.

Mulch also helps control weeds, though my ornamental plants are so close together that weeds have trouble gaining a toehold. There are short annual weeds in some of the beds, but I regard them as additional ground cover. I have occasional perennial weeds, such as goldenrod and pokeweed, but very few. My worst weeds are poison-ivy seedlings, which germinate from seeds in the droppings of songbirds. Still, it takes me only a few hours of weeding once a year to clean up roughly an acre of gardens.

I water very little, except in the case of a newly planted garden. I strongly advise giving a new garden an inch of water once a week for the first year. After the first year, I water only a few plants: astilbes, Japanese irises and ferns. I like the effect the water lovers make and am willing to move hoses to keep them happy.

I firmly believe the old gardening adage about making the fall garden look as you want to find it in the spring. In late fall, I cut everything to within 2 in. of the ground, and leave the trimmings as mulch. I use a good pair of clippers and a hedge trimmer, both battery-operated, and can do all the gardens in one afternoon. (At one time, I used a brush cutter, but its power and noise scared me.) I chop tall plants down by starting at the top and cutting the stems into 6-in. segments, which won't hamper the emergence of my spring bulbs. I don't carry trimmings out of the garden, though it's recommended for plants such as peonies and phlox to prevent diseases from overwintering in the garden and attacking the plants year after year. I haven't seen diseases increase in my gardens.

A final word

I suppose crowded gardens could eventually become overcrowded, but mine haven't. I let the ground covers mat through everything, but I've never allowed the taller perennials to intertwine, mainly because I constantly divide and replant them in yet another new garden. Someday I may have the whole yard planted and then the daylilies and hostas will fight it out in the weeping-willow shade garden. But even that will work out. I have visited a number of overgrown, neglected and even abandoned gardens where the strongest plants—the peonies, Siberian irises, gas plants and daylilies (among others)—are still thriving. Their tenacity is a testimonial for crowding perennials—if abandoned gardens bloom, tended gardens will, too. □

Nancy Carney gardens in Newtown, CT.

Illustration: Laura B. Goodwin

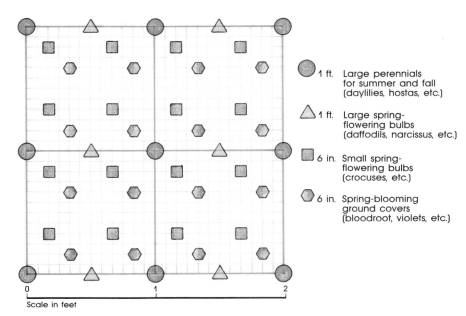

○	1 ft.	Large perennials for summer and fall (daylilies, hostas, etc.)
△	1 ft.	Large spring-flowering bulbs (daffodils, narcissus, etc.)
▢	6 in.	Small spring-flowering bulbs (crocuses, etc.)
⬡	6 in.	Spring-blooming ground covers (bloodroot, violets, etc.)

0   1   2
Scale in feet

Crowded spacing

Author Carney spaces plants by size in her crowded perennial gardens. The grid shown here represents her guidelines. The spacings are regular for clarity; in the garden, Carney plants by eye. She adapts the spacing between plants of the same species for best effect. For example, she sets hibiscus—large, showy plants—5 ft. apart. If the lower-left circle on the grid were a hibiscus, the next four circles in any direction would be different tall perennials.

By May, the garden has filled in luxuriantly. The narcissus leaves in the foreground will soon die back. At center and top, English bluebells (*Endymion non-scriptus*) flower in white and violet. At lower right is a royal fern (*Osmunda regalis*), and near the top is a Goldie's fern (*Dryopteris Goldiana*) with a hosta to its right.

A changing display of showy flowers (above) fills the author's small garden for months. Nearly 200 varieties of bearded iris, such as this tall purple and white one, and flowers like pink sea thrift (left foreground) and magenta columbine (right foreground) take over after the early bulbs are spent.

Tulips such as these cottage varieties (left), along with other bulbs, are some of the earliest bloomers. Other perennials flower in succession, producing concentrated color all season.

Continuous Flower Color from Spring to Fall

Smart choices make the difference

by John W. (Jack) Smith

From late March, when the first crocuses push through the snow, to around mid-October, when the last toad lily dies back, my garden is a constantly changing flower display. Year after year our many visitors ask my wife, Anita, and me, "How do you manage to have a garden that is always full of colorful flowers?"

Creating striking displays of color throughout the growing season is easier than it might seem. And you don't need acres of land or a large crew of helpers to do it. My garden, about half of an average-sized city lot (65 ft. × 130 ft.), is home to a wealth of flowers. Even gardens much smaller than this one can provide all-season color.

Continuous color does not mean that everything in the garden is in bloom all of the time. Rather, enough plants are flowering at any one time to create an impression of sustained color throughout the garden. Here in southwestern Michigan, I've concentrated on plants that bloom from early spring to late fall, letting the garden (and me) have a brief rest the rest of the year. In milder climates, you could easily extend the season of bloom.

Over the past 40 years, I've learned practical ways to choose and combine plants to produce a succession of bright colors for nearly eight months. Using plants that are star performers in your area, you can apply my ideas to make your own long-blooming garden.

Plant choice

Choose a wide assortment—Perennials are the backbone of my garden, but the ones I grow bloom for an average of only three weeks, so I supplement them with annuals, biennials, bulbs, vines, rock garden and container-grown plants, plus a few shrubs and trees. The result is a colorful display for several months. Such a diverse collection inevitably includes plants of different sizes and shapes, which can be tucked in and around each other, so I can pack a surprising number of plants into a small space.

My garden looks quite different today from how it looked initially. At first, I planted my favorite flowers. Once I saw how they performed, I discarded those that proved to be too much work, didn't have a neat growth habit, became too invasive or didn't meet my expectations in other ways.

Select plants for successive bloom—Figuring out when plants bloom in your area is one of the most important steps in planning a long season of color. Depending on the weather and a myriad of other factors, the bloom period can vary considerably from year to year, but you can still use it as a guide, selecting a palette of plants that flower in succession.

At this stage of planning, you might find it useful to make a list of possible plants to grow, grouping them according to time of bloom and kind of plant—annual, perennial, shrub—as well as flower color and height. These things will help you as you design. If you know from the outset that certain plants are not well-suited to your garden—by virtue of their size, growth habit, lack of hardiness or extreme susceptibility to diseases or pests—don't include them.

The best place to start gathering information about bloom time is from knowledgeable people at a local nursery. Because of their experience, they can pinpoint when plants flower in your area, so their information is much more reliable than what you would learn from mail-order nursery catalogs or books, which generally serve a wider geographic area. Too often I've read that a particular plant blooms for ten weeks, only to find its flowering season is much shorter in Michigan. Local garden clubs, neighborhood gardeners and your local university

In early July, white, orange and pink lilies take center stage, replacing astilbes, a few of whose deep pink, feathery flowers still stand in the background. Close spacing and careful plant placement create a striking effect, and island beds make maintenance easy.

Cooperative Extension Service office also may be able to help.

Whatever your source, refine the information with observations from your own garden. Conditions can vary dramatically, even within a few miles. According to the USDA hardiness map, my garden is in Zone 5, but a warmer microclimate allows me to successfully grow some Zone 6 plants. By recording the dates when flowering begins and ends for each kind of plant, I have a handy reference for future planning.

Punctuate the season with periods of peak bloom—One way to whittle down the list of possibilities even further is to plant large numbers of a few groups of plants that bloom one after another, for a changing display from month to month. In my garden, I rely on five groups of plants that flower in succession: tulips and other Dutch bulbs, bearded iris, astilbes, lilies and daylilies. By planting different cultivars or varieties of each, I can stretch out each period of peak bloom.

Any plants that bloom one after another and for which a number of cultivars are available could be substituted for those I've chosen. Early-flowering wildflowers are a good alternative to tulips and other bulbs. Peonies can replace iris, and asters or mums will work in place of late-season daylilies. The longer each plant flowers, the more mileage you'll get out of it, but as long as you select a broad assortment of plants, some of which bloom each month of the growing season, you'll be well on the way to creating continuous color.

The following description of my favorite peak bloomers should give you an idea of how my approach works. Keep in mind that these bloom times are for southwestern Michigan. In the extreme South, the same plants can bloom six to eight weeks earlier, while farther north, flowering may be delayed two to three weeks.

The earliest peak performers to open in my garden are tulips and other spring bulbs, blooming from about April 10 to May 15. During this time, my garden is dotted with every color of the rainbow, from deep red to pure white. The early botanical tulips open first, followed in a week or two by Fosterana, Kaufmanniana and single, early tulips. Accompanying them are crocus, squill (*Scilla* spp.), glory-of-the-snow (*Chionodoxa* spp.), fumewort (*Corydalis bulbosa*), winter aconite (*Eranthis hyemalis*), snowdrop (*Galanthus* spp.) and *Puschkinia*. Next come small-flowered daffodils, *Anemone blanda*, snowflake (*Leucojum* spp.), spring starflower (*Ipheion uniflorum*) and many late-flowering tulips.

From about May 20 to June 10, attention turns to 165 different varieties of bearded iris and a smaller number of *Iris pumila*, a dwarf species. They provide a fine show of nearly every color imaginable. In early July, there is a less extensive, but still-striking, display of white- and purple-flowered Japanese iris.

Just as the bearded iris finish blooming, 150 astilbes fill the garden with their red, pink, magenta, salmon and creamy white flowers. By growing so many cultivars, I've extended their season to July 8, with some of the dwarf types blooming into September.

Complementing the astilbes, 145 varieties of true lilies (*Lilium*) form a tapestry of color from June 20 to July 10. They look quite stately rising above the feathery astilbe flowers. The majority of my lilies are Asiatic and Aurelian hybrids; the rest are Oriental hybrids and species. Most of the Asiatic hybrids range from 2 ft. to 3 ft. tall with up-facing flowers, while the Aurelians reach 5 ft. to 8 ft., with trumpet-shaped, very fragrant flowers. The flowers of the Oriental hybrids are usually white with red or pink markings and a very spicy fragrance.

Before the last lilies have faded, the daylilies (*Hemerocallis*) take over. Their season begins around July 4, peaks between July 10 and 22, and continues into August. With 258 varieties, the garden is especially vibrant at this time. Since there are about 30,000 registered cultivars, your daylily garden can boast every color imaginable except a true blue. Choose from red, pink, salmon, lavender, peach, melon,

yellow, orange and near-white, as well as blended tones and bicolors.

Of the many other flowering plants I grow, some bloom before or after the peak bloomers, while others bloom simultaneously. Annuals, such as fibrous begonias (*Begonia* × *semperflorens*), extend color into September and October, when most of the perennials have finished flowering.

Plant arrangement

My feelings about garden design are summed up by Henry Mitchell in *The Essential Earthman*: "The gardens that look most right are usually small yards presided over for some years by a

Anemone sylvestris 'September Charm' adds a delicate note to the fall garden.

gardener who is not thinking very much of design in any abstract or formal way, but who is exercised over how to grow his favorite plants as well as he can." That said, I do arrange and rearrange plants in my garden until they look pleasing, always aiming to enhance the impression of overall color and to minimize my work.

Plant intensively—With such a small garden, but an ever-growing appetite for new varieties, I've had to grow more than one plant in a given space. Some of my friends have suggested that I must be planting in layers. That's somewhat of an exaggeration, but there are very few bare spots in my garden. I've mostly accomplished this by closely spacing plants

with different bloom times. For example, I've planted early-blooming bulbs and wildflowers right next to iris, astilbes and lilies, which camouflage the early-flowering plants as they begin to die back.

Repeat groupings of the same plants throughout the garden—To create a bigger impact, most perennials are best planted in small groupings of the same genus or of similarly colored flowers, and in more than one place around the garden. Doing so creates splashes of color everywhere. I usually cluster no more than three to six plants together. Large gardens can accommodate more plants per group, but in a small garden, a massive group of the same plants appears shopworn once the flowers have faded.

I make an exception for iris and daylilies, which I plant singly. This enables me to grow many more varieties, and the expanding clumps eventually create a noticeable display. Likewise, robust perennials, such as pink-flowered bachelor's-button (*Centaurea dealbata*), purple coneflower (*Echinacea purpurea*), oxeye daisy (*Heliopsis scabra*) and mallow rose (*Hibiscus moscheutos* 'Disco Belle') are large enough to make a nice showing as single specimens.

Separate plants that bloom at the same time—Rather than planting everything that blooms at the same time in close proximity, distribute the May-bloomers, June-bloomers, and so on, around the garden. The result is flowers in all parts of the garden every month of the growing season. They also draw the eye through the garden, creating the appearance of an uninterrupted expanse of color.

In deciding what to grow where, be bold with color combinations. Nature doesn't worry about whether pink flowers grow next to red or orange ones, and neither should you. I've yet to see colors that really clash.

Plant in island beds—I prefer to plant in "island" beds, distinct planting areas that are readily accessible from more than one side. Surrounded by paths or lawn, these beds are much easier to maintain than deep borders and allow me to appreciate my flowers from several vantage points. Make beds large enough to support a variety of plants, but small enough so you can easily reach everything.

To give the impression of a larger

island, you can cluster several smaller ones together and separate them with paths. Alongside fences, borders do serve a purpose, as long as they're narrow enough to be reached from the front to the back.

Care

Because I don't plant more than I can care for, I've been able to keep my garden work to a minimum. To keep the soil in good shape, I mulch with shredded leaves each fall. I leave them on the garden year-round, and I top-dress with compost during the summer, if needed. I also apply granular fertilizer in the spring. The mulch and dense planting keep most weeds from gaining a foothold and reduce the need for irrigation. Deadheading spent flowers and dividing the astilbes, irises and daylilies are regular tasks. Some of the other perennials require division occasionally. □

John W. Smith gardens in Grand Rapids, Michigan.

A bold combination of pink and red, shade-loving New Guinea impatiens is as at home in this garden as are more toned-down pairings of muted pastel colors.

Daylilies are the midsummer highlight. They start flowering around the Fourth of July and continue into August. Here, their lemony flowers complement the yellow, daisy-like flowers of rudbeckia 'Goldsturm.'

Herbs, tomatoes and chile peppers, chosen for their beauty and flavor, intermingle with purely ornamental flowers in a small edible landscape. By combining attractive edible and ornamental plants, you can have a good-looking garden and reap a tasty harvest.

Edible Landscaping
Gardens to please the palate and the eye

by Nancy Beaubaire

Imagine pausing on the way to your front door and plucking a crisp, juicy apple fresh from a tree in your yard. Or perhaps you stop to munch on a few of the intensely sweet alpine strawberries lining the front walk. You might even be tempted to graze on the red and green ruffly lettuces nestled among bright flowers just behind the berry

plants. All the while, you enjoy the ornamental shrubs, trees and flowers that make your yard a landscape.

That's edible landscaping at its best, a design approach in which attractive food plants are integrated with ornamentals, rather than planted separately (often in the backyard), hidden from the view of passersby. An artfully designed edible landscape, or foodscape, looks ornamental. The only thing that might tip off the neighbors will be your smile of satisfaction as you sample the fruits of your labor.

Why bother growing food in the land-

scape? If you plant the most beautiful edible plants, your garden can look as attractive as a conventional landscape and supply you with flavorful food, at no extra cost in money, water or other resources. As a bonus, you'll have a chance to try new or uncommon vegetables, fruits and herbs, since many of the best-looking edibles, such as pink-fleshed apples or royalty purple pod beans, are rarely found in supermarkets.

Food plants range widely in their appearance, and some I wouldn't include in an edible landscape, although I love

Photo: Rosalind Creasy

Highly decorative cabbages grow amidst drifts of 'Lemon Gem' and 'Tangerine Gem' marigolds whose citrusy, edible flowers are a tasty addition to salads. Here, Jan Blüm, owner of Seeds Blüm, a mail-order nursery in Boise, Idaho, tends her crop.

how they look in my vegetable garden and on my plate. Pumpkins, for example, are too coarse and sprawling to my eye, and Brussels sprouts are too gangly. But in the end, choosing edible ornamentals, as the most attractive of these plants have been dubbed, is a personal matter. Plant those that appeal to you.

A bit of history

The idea of edible landscaping surfaced in the early 1970's. A new generation of gardeners sought to marry the two worlds of gardening—ornamentals and food. Like many gardeners, I felt the need first-hand. I questioned the seemingly artificial division between ornamentals and food plants. Who says, for example, that flowering dogwoods are beautiful, but apple trees aren't? Or that honeysuckle is lovelier than grapevines laden with fruit? What's more, for many urban and suburban dwellers, a dual-purpose planting seemed to make better use of limited space.

I initially became intrigued with the potential of using food plants in the landscape in the early days of edible landscaping when I lived in California. By day, I earned my living designing, planting and caring for residential ornamental landscapes. In the evenings and on weekends, I tended the food garden in my small backyard, a jam-packed collage of vegetables, herbs, flowers and fruit. During the many pleasant hours I spent in my home garden, I couldn't help but notice the beauty of the food plants. Many of them were every bit as striking as the California lilacs, African daisies or lantana I planted for my clients. For several seasons, I planted attractive combinations of food plants and flowers in my own garden: a trellis of bright red-flowered scarlet runner beans underplanted with golden thyme; a tapestry of lettuces and Japanese greens accented by sunny orange poppies and bright blue bachelor's-buttons; native red currants with sweet woodruff and bleeding hearts beneath.

When I was convinced of the landscape-worthiness of edible ornamentals, I began slipping some of these food plants into designs for my clients. A persimmon or plum tree, instead of a magnolia, created a shady sitting area. A ground cover of strawberries substituted for ivy. Kiwi or grapevines, rather than a trumpet vine, cloaked an arbor.

My goal was to blend these handsome food plants harmoniously with purely ornamental plants. If a landscape began to look more like a farm than an ornamental planting, I knew I had gone too far.

Guidelines for success

After years of planting food plants and ornamentals side-by-side and swapping stories with friends in all parts of the country who've done the same, I've realized that edible landscapes are not an all-or-nothing affair. You can plant just a few edible ornamentals, or you can plant lots of them; you can integrate edible ornamentals with your ornamental landscape plants or incorporate them into an attractively designed vegetable or herb garden. In all

The tantalizing orange fruit of 'Hachiya', an Oriental persimmon, makes a striking highlight against the tree's gray bark.

My favorite edible ornamentals

Fruit:

Alpine strawberry—tiny berries, intensely sweet flavor

Oriental and American persimmons (see photo above)

Vegetables:

Scarlet runner beans—edible red flowers and green beans

Red oakleaf lettuce—crimson/burgundy leaves

'Merveille des Quatres Saisons'—lettuce with red-tipped leaves and green hearts

Herbs:

All have edible leaves and flowers.

Chives—green leaves, lavender-pink flowers

Lemon thyme—golden leaves, white flowers

'Purple Ruffles' basil—purple leaves, lavender-to-rose flowers

Tri-color sage—purple, green, cream leaves; lavender flowers

Flowers:

Borage—sky-blue flowers

Nasturtiums—red, rose, orange, salmon, yellow, mahogany flowers; also edible leaves and seed pods

'Lemon Gem' marigolds (See photo p. 63) —N.B.

cases, you'll be rewarded with bounty and beauty. Let me offer you a few guidelines for getting started.

Start with edible ornamentals that you really love to eat. If they happen to require more care than a purely ornamental plant would, you'll be more willing to make the extra effort. And the rewards at harvest time will encourage you to continue growing edibles in your landscape.

Look for the most ornamental cultivars, and choose only those that are well-adapted to your climate. If you're growing lettuce, for example, skip the iceberg and try a velvety green butterhead or a cultivar with ruffly red or glossy green and red-tinted leaves.

Start small. If you've never grown food before, I recommend that you plant only 10% of your landscape in edibles. You can always expand. If you're more experienced, go for more.

RESOURCES

For more information about edible landscaping, consult the following books:

The Beautiful Food Garden by Kate Rogers Gessert. *Storey Communications, Inc., Pownal, VT 05261; 1987. $12.95, paperback; 264 pp.*

The Complete Book of Edible Landscaping by Rosalind Creasy. *Sierra Club Books, 730 Polk St., San Francisco, CA 94109; 1982. $25.00, hardcover; $19.95, paperback; 279 pp.*

Designing and Maintaining Your Edible Landscape Naturally by Robert Kourik. *Metamorphic Press, P.O. Box 1841, Santa Rosa, CA 95402; 1986, $25.00 (includes shipping and handling), paperback; 370 pp.*

The author recommends these mail-order nurseries, which carry a good selection of ornamental edibles:

The Cook's Garden, P.O. Box 535, Londonderry, VT 05148, 802-824-3400. Catalog $1.

Edible Landscaping, P.O. Box 77, Afton, VA 22920. 800-524-4156. Catalog free.

Ornamental Edibles, 3622 Weedin Court, San Jose, CA 95132. Catalog $2.

Seeds Blüm, Idaho City Stage, Boise, ID 83706, 208-342-0858. Catalog $3.

Shepherd's Garden Seeds, 30 Irene St., Torrington, CT 06790. 203-482-3638 or 403-335-6910. Catalog $1.

Balance the proportion of annuals, perennials and woody plants. Your climate will, in part, dictate the optimum mix. If you garden where winters are harsh, include more edible trees and shrubs, which will provide some visual structure during the dormant season, and fewer annuals and herbaceous perennials. In California, I could rely on the many herbaceous perennial or annual edibles that flourish nearly year-round there, but here in Connecticut, the same plants wither to the ground during the winter and would leave giant gaps in the landscape if I devoted too much space to them.

Keep the number of high-maintenance plants that you grow in your landscape to a minimum. Annual edibles, whether they are vegetables, herbs or flowers, are often more labor intensive than most fruit and nut trees or shrubs. Cultivars that are highly susceptible to insect pests and diseases in your area will also probably need more attention, so choose resistant cultivars or substitute a different edible.

Those edibles that do require more attention, such as edible podded peas, should be planted closer to the house—you're more likely to notice them there, and it will be more convenient to tend and harvest them.

Using pesticides in a edible landscape is problematic. Historically, most edible-landscape practitioners haven't used synthetic, highly toxic pesticides, in part because of concern about the risks of harmful residues on their food or in the environment. Also, many pesticides labeled for ornamentals are not permitted on food crops, and when you're growing these plants together, it can be difficult or impossible to spray only the ornamentals. Don't use any pesticide in your edible landscape unless it's labeled for food crops.

Edible flowers can be gorgeous additions to an edible landscape (and to your meals), but be cautious about eating them. Not all flowers are edible, and not all edible flowers are tasty enough to be worth eating. Check in one of the books listed with the Resources at left for more information. Individuals can be sensitive to certain edible flowers, as well, so I recommend that you sample a small amount first and wait a few hours to gauge your reaction before you try more.

Finally, I encourage you to have fun with edible landscaping. Play with different color and texture combinations and indulge your culinary whims. I think you'll be pleased with the results. □

Nancy Beaubaire is managing editor of Fine Gardening *and teaches edible landscaping workshops.*

Photo: Rosalind Creasy

Garden Rooms
Variety makes a small yard big

by Orene Horton

When we bought our house in 1978, the state of the "garden" could have been viewed as a huge problem or a grand opportunity. The backyard was little more than a dirt parking lot; wonderful old camellias overwhelmed the house and blocked many windows; and the front yard was only a boring stretch of grass from foundation planting to curb. Five 60-year-old trees cast dense shade over the long, narrow lot.

A landscape architect helped us to see that dividing the yard into garden rooms—distinctive, separate areas—could give us the illusion of more space. As we've added the plants of our choice over the years, that original organization has served us well.

A fence, mixed border and curving brick path make the author's front yard a garden room. (Photo taken at A on site plan, p. 67.)

A feeling of privacy
When we started the garden, we needed privacy. For one thing, neighbors are close to our 60 ft. × 150 ft. property here in Columbia, South Carolina. What's more, before we could add plants, we had to remove some. To open up space, we sacrificed a deodar cedar in front and two of three huge pecan trees in back.

Behind the house, we saved a hedge of old camellias on the back property line, and planted clematis (the evergreen *Clematis armandii*) to cover one neighbor's chain-link fence. On the west side of the property we erected a brick wall.

To give a sense of enclosure to the front garden without walling it in, we replaced the old, straight driveway with one that curves inward, allowing room for a shrub border on the property line, echoed by a similar bed on the other side. In the high shade of a Darlington oak, salvaged camellias and azaleas, plus gardenia, daphne, rhododendron and several kinds of hydrangeas

grow happily, underplanted with spring-flowering bulbs. To make the front garden seem wider, we tore out the straight-up-the-middle path to the front door and laid a brick path that curves across the width of the yard and leads through a gate to a side garden and path to the backyard.

As my interest in plants grew, I couldn't help eyeing all that grass in the front yard. I have nothing against grass, but one needs only enough perfectly maintained turf to serve as a foil for other plantings. I also wanted to finish enclosing the property by creating a courtyard effect out front, so about four years ago I designed a new bed along the street. (See photo above.) I installed a wrought iron fence and planted a narrow bed on the street side with dwarf Japanese Helleri holly, variegated aspidistra, spring bulbs and hostas. On the house side, I planted a deep, curving bed. Edged with a brick mowing strip, it is anchored by boxwoods and two small trees—a Japanese maple with variegated green-and-cream leaves edged with pink in the spring (*Acer palmatum* 'Butterfly') and a double-flowered star magnolia (*Magnolia stellata* 'Royal Star'). Deciduous shrubs, perennials, annuals and bulbs provide seasonal changes of color. The view from all our front windows is now much more private and interesting.

A suite of rooms
The backyard is divided into four different garden rooms. The first is our outdoor entertainment area, a spot of lawn bordered by brick paths that widen in several places to accommodate tables and chairs. Flower beds line the perimeter. The remaining pecan tree, limbed up high, shades this area. A small pool and fountain tucked into a corner greet you with the sound of water as you enter on the path from the front yard.

Shrubs beneath an outstretched oak enclose the front yard and screen the view of the street. The view from the second floor (below) shows the remaining lawn—small, yet big enough to serve as a cool foil for the brick and for the more colorful flowers. (Photos taken at B and C.)

A second garden room can be glimpsed through an opening in a hedge that is framed by two brick columns topped with a cypress beam. (See p. 68.) A bench in the background beckons. I designed this area as a sitting garden to replace what used to be our children's play area. It is planted mainly with whites and cool pastels—white tulips in spring, white roses in summer underplanted with lamb's ears and rue, and sweet autumn clematis that scrambles over the back wall and shrubs to bloom in a fragrant froth of tiny white flowers in late summer. A hedge of laurustinus viburnum (*Viburnum tinus*) clipped to the same height as the 8-ft. columns encloses this garden. The back wall is formed by a line of old *Camellia sasanqua*, whose fragrant, pale pink blossoms invite you to sit and enjoy the welcome cool weather in fall.

My husband Tate built the brick columns that frame the entrance to this garden as well as the brick edging around the planting beds. He probably regrets having ever signed up for the bricklaying course at the local technical college, because I always have a new project to occupy his weekends. After years of dreaming, this spring we finally added two feet to the height of our 5-ft. garden wall, but Tate was spared—we contracted out

that project. At last I have a wall high enough to support large, climbing roses mingled with clematis. I can hardly wait for them to grow!

An elegant, white birdhouse across the driveway, glimpsed through a honeysuckle-covered arbor in a picket fence, draws you through the gate to a third small room. Although this is the service area, there are beds on either side of the driveway planted for a cottage garden effect with roses, daisies, phlox, coneflowers, and a couple of clumps of ornamental grass. By the back door, I grow a few herbs in a small, sunny bed. Finally, I have a raised bed for starting seeds and cuttings and a compost pile in one last small, concealed area between the garage and the property line.

Containers allow me to grow still more plants. A large collection of pots decorates my back steps. Smaller pots contain sedums, which thrive in spite of our hot summers. I fill larger pots with cascading blue plumbago, pale pink and white fibrous begonias, variegated ivies, white *Zinnia linearis*, and annual vinca, *Catharanthus roseus*. In the fall I plant blue and white pansies over tulip bulbs. Large, painted whiskey barrels by the picket fence gate contain impatiens and variegated ivy in summer and pansies and tulips in spring. The window boxes outside our breakfast room are filled with similar combinations.

Giving a collection unity

An avid collector with a small garden must deal with the problem of how to work in a lot of different plants and still maintain a cohesive design. I have found that it fosters unity to repeat certain key plants and building elements throughout the garden. For example, boxwood (the small evergreen shrub) does well for me. I have used it as background material in front and back, in planters and as a featured plant in several mixed borders. Camellias and Indica azaleas are repeated in several locations. And ivy is everywhere. It clothes the walls on at least three sides of the house and fills a bed under a white crape myrtle at the front entrance. Hydrangeas, hostas, ferns and nandina (heavenly bamboo) also repeat. Tender evergreen shrubs, vines and perennials that do well here—fatsia, pittosporum, aspidistra, Confederate jasmine, and holly ferns—give a sense of structure in winter as well as a feeling of continuity.

I also repeat building materials: brick for paving, walls, columns and bed edgings; wrought iron for fences, porch railings and gates. The white of the house trim repeats in the picket fence, arbor, garage, and birdhouse. Charleston green is used on all the ironwork (gates, porch railings, dining furniture, rose arch) and many painted, concrete pots. I never add anything new

to the design without first considering how compatible it will be with what is already here. With the strong sense of order afforded by all these elements, plantings can be varied and exuberant and still seem perfectly composed.

Mixing plants, matching conditions

Because I have a small lot with two large trees, I've had to adapt my plantings to shade. It's hard to grow grass under large trees, and a sandy soil and a hot climate compound the problem. Fortunately, there are many plants that will thrive in shade if given good soil and enough water. Liberal additions of compost help with the first requirement, and a sprinkler system helps me keep up with water demands. Under my large oak tree, for example, I enriched the soil with lots of compost and created a mixed planting of oakleaf hydrangeas, holly ferns, hostas, wild ginger, hellebores, variegated Solomon's seal, rohdea, Japanese painted fern, and even some cyclamen and primroses, all bordered by variegated liriope. This bed requires no more water or care than grass does, but it has interesting textures and color all year.

The last and most enjoyable part of designing a garden is choosing plants. Over the years I've kept careful records of what does well in my garden and when different plants bloom. My garden diary has helped me to plan for complementary seasonal displays and to avoid repeating mistakes. No more late red camellias blooming beside magenta azaleas! I enjoy designing beds for interesting combinations of foliage and texture, such as hostas with ferns and aspidistra, and I enjoy combining the colors of foliage and flowers to good effect. I like the purple-leaved barberry, *Berberis thunbergii* 'Rose Glow', underplanted with the chartreuse-leaved form of creeping Jenny, *Lysimachia nummularia* 'Aurea', and the hot pink aster 'Alma Potschke'.

I'm mad about variegated plants. They are so effective in shade, where they seem to pull in a touch of sunlight. I especially love the variegated form of *Hydrangea macrophylla* 'Mariesii' with its delicate blue, lacecap

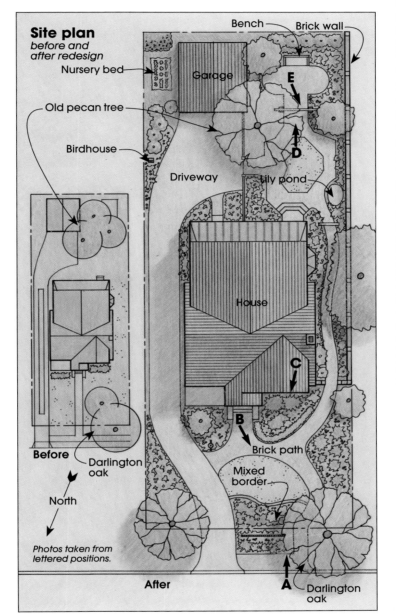

Site plan
before and after redesign

Nursery bed

Old pecan tree

Birdhouse

Bench — Brick wall

Garage

E

D

Driveway — Lily pond

House

C

Before

Darlington oak

North

Photos taken from lettered positions.

B

Brick path

Mixed border

A — Darlington oak

After

blooms. (See facing page.) For containers, nothing makes a better underpinning than a variegated ivy such as 'Glacier', which combines well with almost any color.

The challenge as well as the joy of gardening in South Carolina's Midlands is to have something in bloom every month of the year. While we are famous for our glorious spring display of dogwoods and azaleas, there are too many other possibilities to allow oneself to succumb to the springtime craze by planting even more of these plants. I enjoy the flowers of Lenten roses (or hellebores) and the fragrant shrub *Daphne odora* in January and February and the flowers of *Camellia sasanqua* from October through December. The beautiful red and white striped blooms of a tree form *Camellia japonica* present their display at my dining room window all through the Christmas holidays. The sweet scent of tea olive, *Osmanthus fragrans*, fills the air many times during the year, and the autumn-flowering cherry, *Prunus subhirtella* 'Autumnalis', blooms practically all winter before its spring show.

Spring comes very early here, and perennials described as midsummer bloomers are often in bloom in May or early June along with all the roses and the remaining cool-season annuals. It's quite a feast while it lasts, but there are many long hot days of summer and early fall ahead. Some gardeners opt for all green and

A pair of brick pillars defines the entry to a small sitting area in the back of the property, the section that once housed the children's play equipment. (Photos taken at D and E on site plan.)

Pillars frame the view from the sitting area, revealing the back of the house, brick paving and a small patch of lawn.

retire to air conditioning, but in most of the U.S., many long-lasting perennials and repeat-blooming garden roses will carry the colors on until autumn.

Over time, I have discovered plants which perform during our summers. Native and improved forms of the perennial verbenas do well here in containers or in the border. Salvias have proved to be a wonderful genus for summer-long interest. They provide many shades of blue, a color that is so necessary for most color schemes. I have several hard-working favorites, among them the intensely blue *Salvia guaranitica*, which continues from summer until frost. It combines beautifully with the delicate white blooms of *Asteromoea mongolica* and any color of rose. *Salvia* × 'Indigo Spires' is an imposing 4 ft. × 4 ft. specimen whose dusky blue blooms are constantly covered with bees. *Salvia forskhalii* repeatedly sends up spikes of white-lipped lavender flowers among the blooms of 'Buff Beauty' rose. Finally, the show is joined in August by the gray-leaved, purple-flowered *Salvia leucantha*, which also continues until frost.

Summer-blooming shrubs and ornamental grasses offer still more possibilities. I adore all the hydrangeas with their extravagant flowers that gradually fade and soften over time. Next I love *Buddleia davidii* in white, pink, wine and purple forms, blooming tirelessly from summer until frost if it is kept deadheaded. The ornamental grasses also contribute grace and form to the perennial borders and bloom at a most welcome time. I favor *Miscanthus sinensis* 'Morning Light' and *Miscanthus sinensis* 'Gracillimus', for their slender, graceful foliage.

I must have roses. But in our climate, finding roses that won't lose their leaves to the fungal disease black spot is a challenge. I've thrown away many more than I've kept, but I'm discovering the ones that can take the heat, hold their leaves, keep on blooming and grow with other plants. The pink blooms of 'Carefree Beauty' repeat many times in a season, and this shrub really does live up to its name. Two yellow floribundas, 'All Gold' and 'Sun Flare', are very disease-resistant, as are 'The Fairy', a pink polyantha, 'Little White Pet', another polyantha, and 'Nearly Wild,' a single, pink floribunda. 'Dortmund', a red climber, has been most successful. Old garden roses offer more possibilities. The delicate pink blooms of 'Nastarana', a Noisette, fill the sitting garden with their perfume. The old climbing tea rose 'Sombreuil' greets me with wonderful fragrance and a showering of pale petals on a path.

It's unwise to become too sentimental about plants. I am still looking for more roses, though I will have to get rid of one to add another. Nothing—well, almost nothing—is sacred. So far, only the oak tree and one pecan tree have escaped my shovel-and-wheelbarrow brigade. My husband says he's sure he's moved every shrub in our garden at least three times. By now I have my plants so well trained that they practically leap out of the ground when the wheelbarrow rolls by. If a plant doesn't work in a combination, or if it looks unhappy, I may move it to a more promising spot or I may give it away. But I won't hesitate to compost it if it doesn't meet expectations. Life is too short, and there are too many wonderful plants waiting to be tried. □

Orene Horton teaches, consults and writes about gardening in Columbia, South Carolina.

Containers of colorful annuals and perennials brighten the back steps of the house and turn pavement into planting space.

Hydrangea macrophylla 'Mariesii' brightens a dark front corner under a mature oak. The white-edged leaves put the shrub among author Horton's favorite variegated plants.

Two planters nest in a broad, deck-like platform at the front door of the house, adding a final welcome to the wooden walkway. Lady's mantle covers itself with yellow flowers in the foreground, and a Japanese maple shelters shade-tolerant perennials in one of the planters.

Entryway Invitation
Design ideas for the route to the front door

by Bruce Crawford

As I slogged around the site, mud stuck to my boots. Nearly complete, the house had been nicely set into a hill, with the front door just above grade. The yard, nearly bare, sloped down to a basement garage. My challenge as a garden designer was to start from nothing and make an attractive landscape with an inviting path to the front door. The design I built for my clients has several features that would work for other front yards: a broad, indirect path with a dramatic beginning and end, a curving wall of stone to break the slope and small, distinct gardens.

A walkway that says "welcome"
I follow a few guidelines when I design a front walkway. For one thing, it should be wide enough so that two people can comfortably stroll side by side. I recommend a width of at least 4 ft., but the ideal is 5 ft. to 6 ft. A path that permits people to walk only single file does not say "Welcome."

Unless the garden is formal, I also try to make the front walk curve and turn so visitors can enjoy changing views of the garden and are drawn ahead by hints of what's to come. But keep the turns moderate or you and your visitors are likely to cut corners.

On a slope, take care with the location and the sequence of the steps. Try to keep every flight of steps under 4½ ft. in height. On tall slopes, I break the path into several flights of steps with level runs between them. By alternating the steps and the path, I make the walkway less arduous and more inviting. For safety, I put all steps within straight runs, not at the turns.

Settling on a design

After some consideration, I decided to make the walkway of wood, borrowing the kind of construction used for decks. The major problem with decks is that high heels get caught in the cracks between planks. To reduce the number of cracks in the walkway, I chose wide planks—2×8's—and oriented them in the same direction as the walkway. I would have liked even wider boards, but I was concerned that they would cup and warp badly as they weathered.

My clients and I decided the entry walk should start at the driveway beside the garage, not at the street. For one thing, guests were most likely to park in the driveway. For another, a path from the street would have run head on and level to the front door, while a path from the driveway would cross the front of the house and climb the slope, offering us a chance to change direction, include steps and add some interesting gardens.

At the front door, I ended the walkway with a wide platform divided into two steps that make a gracious and attractive entrance. I incorporated two planters in the platform for an entryway garden, and planted them with shade-tolerant perennials and a cultivar of fullmoon maple (*Acer japonicum* var. *laciniatum*) called 'Aconitifolium' (see photo on facing page). The maple, which will not outgrow its spot, makes a distinctive accent with its unusual, hand-shaped leaves.

At the other end, I split the walkway in two, with one fork stepping down to the garage and the other continuing straight to the driveway. Between the forks, I set a wooden planter sheathed with cedar siding to match the house.

A walkway of wood

The walkway is actually a series of decks on short posts that rest on concrete footings. The only really tricky part of construction was laying out the footings. I found that the easiest and most accurate method was to stake the corners of the walk, stretch string between the stakes, and drop down from the string to locate the footings. Much of the front yard was 1 ft. to 4 ft. of freshly spread fill; I knew it would settle eventually, so the footings had to be solid. I dug the holes to a depth of 30 in. in the shape of an inverted cone in order to distribute the load downward and outward. After five years, the walkway shows no signs of settling.

Each run of the walkway is a box with inset decking and mitered corners so no ends are visible. The maximum span between posts is 10 ft., with most runs no greater than 8 ft. The boxes are made of 2×8's; 2×6's inside them support the decking so it sits level with the tops of the 2×8's. I ran joists on 16 in. centers across each box, and nailed the 2×8 decking with ten-penny oval-headed siding nails, which have a neater appearance than common nails.

The steps took a lot of work because I ran the decking in the same direction as the path and made the risers 7 in. high and the treads 14 in. wide instead of the standard 8 in. and 12 in. I assembled stairstep-shaped supports for the sides and middle of the steps and then nailed 2×6's between the supports to carry the decking.

All lumber, with the exception of the cedar siding on the planter, is CCA pressure-treated southern yellow pine, which is sold at most lumberyards. [For more on pressure-treated lumber, see *FG* #18, pp. 68-71.] I stained the walkway, steps and planter gray to match the house. The walkway has been restained once, a few boards that cupped excessively were replaced, and I have not heard of any guests losing high heels. Unfortunately, a few woodchucks set up homes under the walkway. The next time, I'll tack chicken wire between the posts.

Laying up stone

I've worked with many types of stone over the years, and I am convinced that flat stones that are roughly 2 in. to 8 in thick—I use broken bluestone—are best for a dry wall (a wall without mortar). Not only is bluestone flat and thin, it does not require much chiseling and shaping, the most time-consuming part of laying walls. Because it's relatively thin, bluestone has one disadvantage: it obliges you to lay up a lot of pieces.

Dry-laid retaining walls should be thicker at the bottom than at the top, and should lean into the slope. I made the wall 3 ft. to 3½ ft. thick at the base and 2 ft. thick at the top. The face leans 3 in. to 4 in. for every 1 ft. of height. I started by excavating a trench 24 in. deep and filling it with 13 in. of compacted ⅜-in. crushed stone. As I laid up the wall, I backfilled behind it with gravel and sand to provide good drainage. I prefer to backfill as the wall goes up, because otherwise the soil behind the wall can slump.

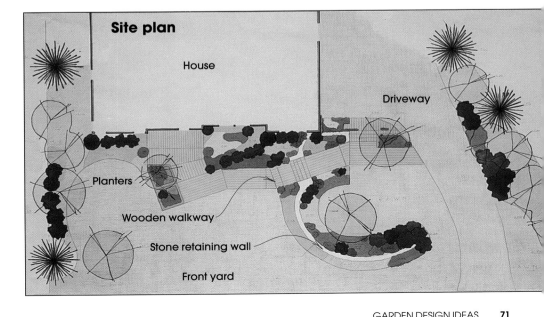

Site plan

House

Driveway

Planters

Wooden walkway

Stone retaining wall

Front yard

Illustration: Bruce Crawford

Broad enough to allow people to stroll two abreast, the wooden walkway changes direction repeatedly for surprise and leads to a flight of steps (hidden in this view) through a stone retaining wall that curves away to the right.

A wooden planter and a low, bluestone wall flank the start of the walkway to the front door. Visitors see two gardens along the walkway, one level with the planter, the other up the flight of stairs in the distance. In the planter, hellebores nestle at the base of a three-stemmed birch tree. (A strong wind blurs parts of the plants.)

The main trick to laying flat stones is to place pieces with similar thickness next to each other so you can seat another stone firmly over the joint. Avoid joints that run up and down for three or more courses; they weaken the wall and look unsettling.

I like to cap a wall with a course of stones that is roughly 24 in. wide so that someone can easily walk along it and view the garden from a different angle. I lay the cap stones in mortar so they will not shift or wobble when walked upon.

A walled garden

As the design of the walkway became clear, I saw a chance to make a walled garden at the driveway end. By cutting a terrace into the slope and building a retaining wall to hold the higher ground, I could add a small, almost-enclosed garden two steps up from the driveway. A tulip tree was in the way, but it was dying, a casualty of misguided earthmoving. The road builders had pushed 4 ft. to 5 ft. of soil over half its roots, smothering them. The tree died in the spring, and I had it cut down.

The retaining wall gives the garden a feeling of privacy and enclosure. It starts 3½ ft. high at the house and curves away toward the street, dropping to 2½ ft. at the other end. The bluestone pieces are roughly 1½ in. thick and predominately blue and gray with some browns, colors that complement the house and walk. The wall has strong, crisp horizontal lines and looks contemporary.

Choosing plants

Density is vital in garden design. If you use a lot of herbaceous perennials, grasses included, the garden needs a backbone of denser, preferably evergreen, plants. The evergreens provide winter interest and hold the garden together year-round while the perennials come into their glory and fade. For the entryway garden, I chose two evergreen shrubs, both under 5 ft. tall, with dark, dense foliage. One was the Oregon grape holly (*Mahonia aquifolium*), which has spiny leaves and clusters of blue berries, and the other was the native mountain laurel (*Kalmia latifolia*), which has smooth, lance-shaped leaves and covers itself with white-to-pink flowers in late spring.

I restricted the design largely to colors that would complement rather than compete with the house. Bright flowers appear only in pots next to the front door and in the walled garden. Since the walled garden is hidden from the street, it provides a burst of unexpected color for the visitor.

Along the top of the retaining wall and beside the house, the predominant colors of the design, aside from green, are blue, silver and white. Blues are provided by catnip (*Nepeta mussinii*), lavender (*Lavandula angustifolia* 'Munstead'), and blue Lyme grass (*Elymus arenarius*). Silver is provided by the leaves of lavender, catnip and snow-in-summer (*Cerastium tomentosum*), which also offers white flowers from May until early June at roughly the same time that the mountain laurel flowers. Most silver-leaved plants require partial sun and well drained soil of low fertility. I had an ideal spot along the top of the retaining wall, since the backfill there was mostly sand and gravel.

Using certain plants repeatedly gives a garden cohesiveness. I decided to repeat blue Lyme grass at the base of the wall and in the planter by the garage. A perennial, blue Lyme grass makes a fountain of narrow, 2-ft. long, blue leaves that are resistant to insects and diseases and look good from spring to winter. Unfortunately, it also tends to be slightly invasive. To keep it in check, you have to pull out adventurous stolons—underground stems— during spring cleanup and several more times during the growing season. I think its looks are worth the effort. In the planter, however, I wanted to curb it completely, so I set it in a 12-in. length of the clay flue pipe used in chimneys. In five years, the plant has not escaped once. It has filled the flue pipe, and will need dividing in the next year or two.

In the walled garden, I added new colors, mainly pinks and yellows. Yellow makes blue more telling and vibrant, so I mixed lady's mantle (*Alchemilla mollis*) and *Coreopsis verticillata* 'Moonbeam' with blue Lyme grass at the foot of the wall. Stronger yellows are supplied by 'King Alfred' narcissus in April, woolly yarrow (*Achillea tomentosa*) in May and *Achillea* 'Coronation Gold' in June and July. In August and September, gaura (*Gaura lindheimeri*), an 18-in., vase-shaped perennial, blooms with white flowers, and in early spring, Lenten rose (*Helleborus orientalis*) and bergenia (*Bergenia purpurascens*) offer pink flowers.

To enliven the retaining wall, I

The yellow flowers of lady's mantle contrast strikingly with the narrow, arching leaves of blue Lyme grass at the foot of a dry-laid bluestone wall. The purple spikes above the wall are lavender.

included tunnels of soil between the stones and planted them with sedum 'Ruby Glow', a small, hardy succulent with purple foliage and pink flowers that fade to bronze. Unfortunately, over half of these plants have died, probably because the tunnels dry up. I've replanted the empty spots with cobweb houseleek (*Sempervivum arachnoideum*), hoping it will prove more drought-tolerant.

The entryway gardens and walkway have been a success. With lavender, lady's mantle, blue Lyme grass and the other perennials filling in nicely, and the woody evergreens providing density and screening, the gardens are inviting. And the wide, solid walkway says "Welcome." □

Bruce Crawford is a garden designer in Andover, New Jersey.

Designing for a Small Side Yard
Color, fragrance, path and patio work together

by Avis Rappoport Licht

It's always a challenge to figure out how to make small gardens work. I try to make any garden, regardless of size, functional, unified and visually interesting. All the components of a garden need to fit its scale. But in a small garden, plants that are very wide or tall appear out of proportion and the garden looks even smaller. Likewise, with too many different plants the garden looks like a hodgepodge, but with too few it's boring. During my 11 years as a landscape designer, I've tackled a lot of small gardens, and though the general problems are similar, I've tried to solve each one differently.

A year ago, Shirley Freriks asked me to plan a garden for the side yard next to her house in Corte Madera, California. I previously had designed and planted a low-maintenance landscape for her hillside front yard, and though it pleased her, it had also given her a better idea of what was lacking in her yard. Most of the front yard was in full view of the neighbors, and it was readily accessible to a large deer population, which drastically limited the variety of flowers she could grow. There was no flat sitting area, although our mild climate is perfect for outdoor living.

Shirley wanted a private place in the side yard where she could sit and enjoy the sun, but she didn't want a lawn. She loves flowers, both for cutting and to admire in the garden, so she had a mind to grow a greater range of plants in the side yard for year-round bloom. Scented flowers, especially roses, appealed to her, so we decided that fragrance would be a wonderful focus for the garden. The side yard is much smaller than the front, so I could include some plants requiring a bit more care and still keep the maintenance down. Most of the plants would be perennials, but Shirley also wanted spots where she could tuck in a few seasonal flowers.

Imagining the new garden was exhilarating, but assessing the site was sobering. The side yard was just 22 ft. by 40 ft., and very steep, with no easy access. The walls of the house towered above it. Part of the yard was hot and sunny, and part was shady. Months of construction work had compacted the clay loam soil, and only a few scraggly plants remained.

Despite its problems, the yard had several assets. It already was almost completely blocked from view, screened by the hillside at the top, woods at the bottom and the house on one side; a low fence ran along part of the other side. The slope offered interesting vantage points for viewing the garden plantings. And the distant Marin County hills, visible above the treetops, created a restful feeling.

Hardscape

I began designing with the hardscape, which is landscape designers' shorthand for everything that isn't plants. I decided to carve three terraces out of the hillside, holding them in place with granite-riprap retaining walls (see site plan, p. 76). This material is an inexpensive, unfaced light-gray stone; generally it's not considered very attractive, but the color complemented Shirley's gray house.

The large lower terrace, in the garden's sunniest and most private spot, is a stone patio, interplanted with blue-star creeper, a ground cover with delicate oval leaves and light-blue flowers from early spring through summer. A narrow path of river-washed stones winds uphill to the front yard, its scale in keeping with the size and private nature of the garden.

The path divides the garden's shady and sunny parts. On the sunny side, two terraces provide planting beds and help control erosion. The slope was steep enough for more than two terraces, but I didn't want the view from the patio dominated by rock walls. The wall separating the patio and first terrace curves, in graceful contrast to the straight lines of the house walls. The second terraced wall, higher up the hill, allowed me to add topsoil to the slope without having to berm it up against the house. The shaded part of the garden was too narrow to effectively terrace, so I decided that low-growing ground covers would have to hold the soil instead.

To deter deer, I added to the existing run of 4-ft.-high picket fence. At the bottom of the garden, the new fence sits on an existing 3-ft.-high retaining wall. Near the top gate, it rests on the ground, so I trained a vine above it to increase its effective height. I trained four photinias as standards in front of the existing section of fence. Their foliage rises about 5 ft. above stems that are bare to the top of the pickets, discouraging the deer and screening the garden while not shading it too much. Most plants that would form a tall screen would be too wide for this narrow planting area. Photinia, however, tolerates pruning well and it grows quickly.

Plantings

For the plantings, I wanted to evoke the feeling of an English cottage garden, where plants meld together impressionistically rather than in a formal layout. In this garden I applied some of the unifying principles I use in larger ones: putting taller plants in the background; massing plants by species, height or color; and repeating some of these groupings in different areas. Here, I used shorter plants, fewer groups and fewer in each group. I also paid special attention to balancing simplicity and variety—too much of a good thing really sticks out in a small area.

Our frost-free climate, with its cool, wet winters and warm, dry summers, is well suited for many different flowering plants. I limited my choices of plants mostly to those that wouldn't grow much taller than 2 ft. to 3 ft., including evergreen flowering shrubs, herbaceous perennials, bulbs and ground covers. Low-growing plants wouldn't dwarf the garden. Even if their foliage or form varied, many plants of a similar height could link the different parts of the garden. I also included some with upright, swordlike foliage. Such plants look taller than they really are, and would create an illusion of greater variation in height in parts of the garden.

I selected a few taller shrubs and climbing vines to help the eye make the transition from the low-growing plants to the otherwise dominating forms of the house and fence behind. If these taller plants were bushy or fast-growing, I made sure I picked ones that could be

In this small side yard, stone steps lead down a slope through a diversity of colorful plants to a patio. The coralbells (left, foreground), swordlike iris leaves and upright flower stalks of lavender add height without overcrowding.

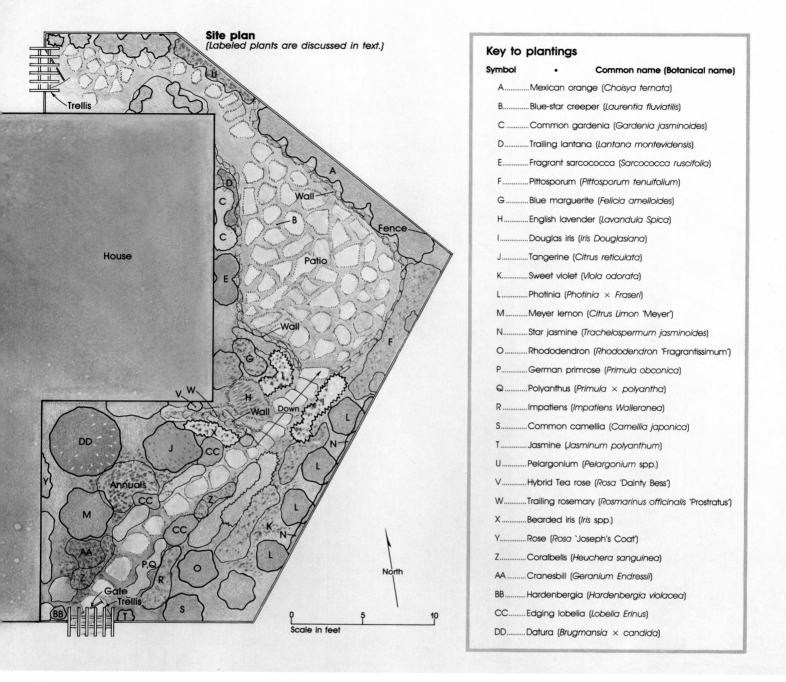

Site plan
(Labeled plants are discussed in text.)

Trellis · House · Wall · Fence · Patio · Wall · Wall · Down · Annuals · Gate Trellis · North

Scale in feet: 0 5 10

Key to plantings

Symbol	•	Common name (Botanical name)
A		Mexican orange (*Choisya ternata*)
B		Blue-star creeper (*Laurentia fluviatilis*)
C		Common gardenia (*Gardenia jasminoides*)
D		Trailing lantana (*Lantana montevidensis*)
E		Fragrant sarcococca (*Sarcococca ruscifolia*)
F		Pittosporum (*Pittosporum tenuifolium*)
G		Blue marguerite (*Felicia amelloides*)
H		English lavender (*Lavandula Spica*)
I		Douglas iris (*Iris Douglasiana*)
J		Tangerine (*Citrus reticulata*)
K		Sweet violet (*Viola odorata*)
L		Photinia (*Photinia × Fraseri*)
M		Meyer lemon (*Citrus Limon* 'Meyer')
N		Star jasmine (*Trachelospermum jasminoides*)
O		Rhododendron (*Rhododendron* 'Fragrantissimum')
P		German primrose (*Primula obconica*)
Q		Polyanthus (*Primula × polyantha*)
R		Impatiens (*Impatiens Walleranea*)
S		Common camellia (*Camellia japonica*)
T		Jasmine (*Jasminum polyanthum*)
U		Pelargonium (*Pelargonium* spp.)
V		Hybrid Tea rose (*Rosa* 'Dainty Bess')
W		Trailing rosemary (*Rosmarinus officinalis* 'Prostratus')
X		Bearded iris (*Iris* spp.)
Y		Rose (*Rosa* 'Joseph's Coat')
Z		Coralbells (*Heuchera sanguinea*)
AA		Cranesbill (*Geranium Endressii*)
BB		Hardenbergia (*Hardenbergia violacea*)
CC		Edging lobelia (*Lobelia Erinus*)
DD		Datura (*Brugmansia × candida*)

kept in bounds by pruning.

In addition to height, I chose plants on the basis of color and fragrance, looking for those with long bloom periods and overlapping flowering times. Shirley's favorite flower colors are lavender, purple, blue, pink and coral, and I stuck mostly with them. They blend nicely, but aren't monotonous. I needed some shade-tolerant plants, and others that would stand full sun. Except for these light requirements, plants with similar cultural needs were almost a necessity; it would demand too much effort in a small garden to create special niches. We treated all the plants alike, mixing composted chicken manure, bone meal and blood meal into each planting hole to provide organic matter,

phosphorus and nitrogen, respectively.

Near the top of the garden, on the sunny side, I planted a tangerine, a Meyer lemon and a datura. All are evergreens with fragrant, white flowers. The citrus grow to about 5 ft. and bloom almost continuously. The datura, which can be kept to 7 ft. with annual hard pruning, blooms heavily in the spring and summer and intermittently the rest of the year. Its heavy, tropical scent earned it a place by the bedroom window. Beneath these is a colorful carpet of lower-growing plants. Freesias, hyacinths and daffodils bloom in February. In spring and summer come Johnny-jump-ups, violas, bachelor's-buttons, dianthus, coralbells, nigellas and tiny geraniums, followed by anemones in the fall.

Across the path on the shady side, the dark-green foliage of a camellia and a fragrant rhododendron mirrors the similar foliage of the citrus and datura. The dark foliage of these plants gives a sense of depth to the shallow space. The pink flowers of the camellia and the white flowers of the rhododendron appear in early spring, along with yellow and cream-colored primroses beneath them. To cover the ground quickly and hold the soil on the unterraced shady side, I planted forget-me-nots, lilies-of-the-valley, lobelias, violas and a few lacy-leaved ferns. Pink impatiens flowers until frost, and complements the pink, lavender and blue flowers of the coralbells, lobelias, violas and Douglas irises growing along

Near the gate (top left), a solid mat of flowers stabilizes the unterraced left side of the slope, while *Jasminum polyanthum* climbs above the fence. White-flowered datura, climbing roses and citrus fill a corner next to the house with fragrance (left). The patio (above), interplanted with blue-star creeper, is a perfect place to sit and enjoy pelargoniums (foreground), and the pink-flowered lantana, blue-flowered marguerite and lavender above the terrace wall. Photinia standards along the fence screen the garden.

the sides of the path. Dichondra anchors the soil around the stepping stones.

Moving down the path to the terrace, mounded shrubs such as rosemary, blue-flowered marguerite and pink-flowered lantana thrive in the hot sun without much water. In contrast are the swordlike leaves of irises and fortnight lilies, the slender flower stalks of lilies-of-the-valley and coralbells, and the spiky stalks of lavender. Just above the patio, sweet alyssum drapes over the wall. Next to it, the dark-green foliage of sarcococca and gardenias holds its own against the house. The white flowers of these plants, along with those of the low border of Mexican orange next to the patio, perfume the air during much of the spring

and summer. Along the fence, four pittosporums join the Mexican orange and the photinia standards, providing some variety there.

Vines appear several places in the garden. *Hardenbergia violacea*, a delicate vine with pea-like, brilliant-purple flowers that bloom in early spring, twines up the fence on one side of the gate. On the other side, *Jasminum polyanthum* climbs a trellis. Its white, fragrant flowers are followed by those of star jasmine, growing farther down the fence beneath the photinias. Near the citrus, two pink-flowered roses cover part of the house walls, their thorny stems well out of the way.

The mature garden is a profusion of color and fragrance all packed into a

small area. The trailing rosemary completely covers the upper wall, and the blue-star creeper is gradually growing up the wall behind the patio. The plants on the shady side have formed a dense ground cover. Under the shrubs, filigree-like flowers rise above a green mat. The stones in the walls, path and patio help to structure and unify the garden. Watering takes little time with an in-ground, low-volume spray system, and fertilizing and pruning require only a few hours a week. Shirley spends much more time than this in her garden, just enjoying the abundance. □

Avis Rappoport Licht is a landscape designer and owns Sweetbriar, a landscaping company in Woodacre, California.

A Courtyard Garden

Symmetry and lush plantings make the most of a small space

A table and chairs in the center of a walled patio provide a cozy place to dine. Four L-shaped flower beds (two visible here) lend symmetry, color and fragrance to this outdoor living area. A fountain beneath the arch of the brick wall serves as a focal point.

by Jane E. Lappin

If you open your mind to the possibilities, a small space can be transformed into a unique and visually rich garden. Sometimes good things do come in small packages.

When my clients asked me to create a garden for their small courtyard, I realized I had a delightful challenge on my hands. Enclosed on three sides by the house and on the fourth by a 10-ft. tall brick wall, the site was ideal for an intimate garden and outdoor living area.

I designed a courtyard garden with principles I've found helpful for small sites. I created planting beds and a

defined sitting area, balanced the garden visually, and packed it with flowers, creating a serene, cozy environment. Many of these features could be adapted to your garden as well.

Planning the garden

Before I design a small garden, I consider how it will be used. My clients were relaxed people with an informal lifestyle. They loved being outside with friends and relatives, and they asked me to develop the courtyard into a flower-filled haven for entertaining, sitting and walking around. My clients also liked the prospect of a small, protected garden—it would be a pleasing contrast to the immensity of the ocean nearby.

I began by taking stock of the site. The courtyard, roughly 25 ft. by 25 ft., was visible from many rooms in the house. I would have to make sure the garden offered attractive views from several perspectives. An existing fountain set in the wall would make a soothing sound as it trickled into a semicircular brick basin below. Beneath the tangle of overgrown plantings in the courtyard, I uncovered a path of bluestone pavers, which I decided to extend throughout the garden.

Before I settled on a final design, I discarded several options. A central sundial and beds edged with clipped hedges would look attractive from inside the house, but would be too regimented for my clients' tastes. A formal design would also restrict use of the garden to that of a passageway. I also thought about an elaborate garden of vegetables, herbs and cutting flowers for "Dad," who loved to cook. While pretty and utilitarian, however, it wouldn't look lush enough all season.

In the end, I decided to make a garden room—an area that serves as an extension of the house. The architecture and interior of the house had an old-world flavor, so I envisioned a garden overflowing with an abundance of flowers, much like those created during the Renaissance in Italy. It should invite, even compel, people to enter, luring them in with its beauty and appealing to all of their senses. There would be no holding back here—the plantings would burst forth, unrestrained by precise border edges or an over-eager pruning shears. Such a design would meet my clients' needs and their tastes, and it would look lovely from inside as well as from outside.

A garden of moods

Once I've decided on an overall design for a garden, I think about how I want it to make people feel. In a small, enclosed garden, no sweeping vistas contribute to the mood, and everything has a greater impact than in a large, open area. For the courtyard, I relied on cool-colored and fragrant plants to convey a feeling of restfulness and romance.

Tall, white-throated delphiniums tower over the purple spikes of blue salvia. The salvia will continue flowering long after the delphiniums are spent, creating a long season of bloom.

Cool colors for a hot area—I planted flowers in shades of pink, blue, lavender, purple or white, colors that soothe the eye and complement, rather than fight, with each other. Restricting the colors encourages the eye to rest. The result is a romantic, gentle atmosphere, even during July and August when the courtyard is sunny and hot.

Leaf color and texture also contribute to the peaceful mood. I wanted the foliage to unify the garden and to blend with the flowers, rather than become the main focus. Silver, blue, purple and variegated leaves look restful and contrast enough with the flowers to be noticed, but not enough to stop your eye. For similar reasons, I avoided leaves with shiny textures or a stiff bearing, and relied instead on leaves with furry, pebbly or dull surfaces. For example, I chose scented geraniums for their downy, medium green leaves; borage for its fuzzy, blue-green, leaves; artemisia for its silvery, smooth leaves, and an ornamental sage for its dull purple, pebbly leaves.

Fragrance—Fragrance creates a mood of romance in the garden. It invites you to visit and linger, drawing you into the garden and then luring you from scent to scent. Each year I try different fragrant plants in the courtyard garden, but I have a few favorites. *Nicotiana* 'White Cloud', a white-flowered annual, grows to about 3 ft. tall and reliably perfumes the nighttime air with heady, rich scent. For August fragrance, I plant single and double flowering tuberoses (*Polianthes tuberosa*). These tender bulbs bear creamy white flowers on 2-ft. tall flower spires that emerge from tall, grasslike foliage. When even the slightest breeze blows, the flowers emit a sweet, light fragrance, reminiscent of a tropical summer night. Since tuberose leaves are not beautiful or substantial enough to warrant a separate stand, and because the flowers bloom so late in the season, I tuck them among earlier-flowering perennials.

A patch of herbs—sage, basil, rosemary, tarragon and spearmint—offers both fragrant foliage and flavors for the kitchen.

The pleasures of symmetry

Symmetry in a garden pleases the eye. When I design a garden, I look first for structural symmetry—for example, paths that divide the garden into equal parts or planting beds on either side of a line of sight. But symmetry need not

Perennials in a perimeter bed gradually rise from low plants at the edge to taller ones in the background. White clary sage in the center is flanked by purple delphinium, magenta loosestrife and maiden grass on the left, pink malva behind and bright pink dahlias on the right.

Cool-colored flowers lend a restful feeling to the garden. Pink and white verbena and magenta verbena 'Lavender Lace' sprawl over the edge of the bed. Behind them (from left to right), the purple spikes of blue salvia, white roses and blue borage nestle together.

have crisp, geometric edges or require carefully trimmed plants; you can also create it by choosing a focal point and planting in graduated heights.

A center for the garden—I decided to center this garden around the view from the living room, with the fountain as the focal point. I planned a sitting and eating area in the middle of the courtyard surrounded by four L-shaped planting beds. Wide paths would separate these beds from narrow ones along the perimeter walls.

I couldn't make the L-shaped beds the same size because one side of the garden was shorter than the other. So, I created an appearance of symmetry by placing the beds the same distance from the fountain, by making them all the same shape, and by planting them as nearly mirror images in color, texture and scale.

I reinforced the illusion of balance in several ways. Plants loosely spill over the edges of the beds and nestle together, which keeps your eye moving. An urn placed at the inner corner of each bed directs the eye away from the outer corner, where the discrepancy in length would be noticeable. The urns also make the fountain look centered along the length of the wall.

Balance with heights—To emphasize the symmetry of the garden, I planted it in graduated heights. Viewed from the sitting area, the plants rise from low-growers (8 in. to 10 in. tall) through those that are mid-height (15 in. to 24 in.) to taller ones (30 in. to 36 in.). The layered look repeats no matter which direction you look, so the garden appears balanced. At 36 in., the tallest plants allow a view of the fountain beyond them and of the perennials in the perimeter beds. I wanted people to feel cuddled and slightly overwhelmed, sensations that are heightened by the tall plants.

There is much going on in the center beds, so I limited the number of varieties along the perimeter. I chose subtle contrasts in flowers and foliage, too. I relied on hearty perennials that I can trust to flower each year. Pink meadowsweet (*Filipendula purpurea* 'Elegans') bears feathery, white flowers in late June. Garden phlox (*Phlox paniculata* 'Bright Eyes'), which has clusters of pink flowers with red eyes, and phlox 'Blue Boy', with its lavender-blue flowers, open from mid-July into August. Two loosestrifes—*Lythrum virgatum* 'Morden Pink', which has rose-pink flower spikes, and 'Purple Spires', which has purple-tinted flowers—fill in quickly without becoming invasive. (Use discretion in planting loosestrife. In some states *Lythrum salicaria*, an invasive loosestrife, and 'Morden Pink', which can become invasive if pollinated by *L. salicaria*, are illegal to grow.)

In the corners of the perimeter beds, I planted maiden grass (*Miscanthus sinensis* 'Gracillimus'), whose white plumes reach 5 ft. With its fine texture and upright arching habit, it adds a touch of gracefulness. For a fun contrast, I placed purple-black hollyhock (*Alcea rosea* 'Nigra'), which reaches 6 ft. and taller, around the grasses.

Overgrowing

To get more flowers from the garden, I used a technique that I've dubbed overgrowing. I plant next to each other

The bright pink flowers of an annual verbena spill from a pedestaled urn. Below the urn, silvery-leaved helichrysum intermingles with the soft green leaves and white flowers of a scented geranium and purple verbena.

two different plants with slightly overlapping bloom times (or nearly so). The earlier-blooming plant dominates the space first. After it flowers, I let it die back naturally or prune it back enough to give more room to its neighbor, which then becomes the focus of attention. I give the later-blooming plant a light feeding once the early bloomer is spent. The plants don't have to physically grow over each other, but in some cases they do. Overgrowing lends itself particularly well to informal gardens, where some blurring of the edges and friendly jostling of plants is acceptable.

Overgrowing can involve any combination of annuals, perennials and biennials. I choose plants that will not crowd, choke or invade their neighbors. The later-blooming plant generally is one that grows slowly in the beginning of the season. For example, I plant delphiniums, which grow fast in spring and flower in June, with blue salvia (*Salvia farinacea* 'Victoria') and purple and pink verbenas. The salvia and the verbenas start slowly and flower after the delphiniums, usually from late June to frost. If I prune the delphiniums hard after they flower, they rebloom later in the season.

I also pair catmint (*Nepeta mussinii*) with verbena 'Cleopatra Pink' and with 'Polaris', a cultivar of lilac verbena (*Verbena rigida*). The catmint, a low-growing perennial with gray-green leaves and lavender-blue flowers, blooms through early summer. Then the verbena has center stage, blooming from late July until frost.

Borage, a self-seeding annual whose dusty blue, star-shaped flowers open in June through late July, is overgrown by dahlias, which bloom from July through August. Borage in full bloom requires plenty of room, but when it's finished, I just prune its foliage way back and let the dahlias take over.

I encourage you to experiment with overgrowing. It takes a bit of know-how and labor, but it's worth the effort and is lots of fun. The garden always appears to be in full bloom. And the plants support each other, so those that ordinarily would require staking need very little.

Jane E. Lappin designs gardens and grows rare and unusual plants in the East Hampton area of Long Island, New York.

Inspired by the great public gardens she visited, the author adapted elements of their design to fit her large farmland property in Maine. A sweeping flower border frames the view to a nearby lake, its informal curves fitting the rural character of the property.

Landscaping a Large Property
Adapting ideas from great estates

by Dianne Hogendorn

A large piece of land offers many gardening opportunities, but little information is available to help gardeners who want to do the work themselves without spending lots of money. When my husband and I first bought an old farm in Maine in the late 1960s, we were ecstatic at the prospect of owning so much land—about 100 acres all told. A mowed lawn occupied a small circle around the house. Beyond it, meadows and forest stretched off in the distance. The land was in quite good condition except for localized ravages of prior lumbering

operations and brush creeping over the stone walls along the meadows' edges. Over time, my husband turned ever-larger sections of meadow into lawn, and I made gardens along the stone walls. Neither of us had any formal knowledge of landscaping or horticulture, yet by restoring order to a farm that would otherwise revert to wilderness, we sensed we were also creating beauty.

As we worked, I turned to gardening books and magazines for ideas. There I found many articles about small enclosed yards designed by homeowners or grand estates designed by professionals, but very little information to help me with such a large lot. In fact, I got the feeling that we were doing something wrong, because I never saw a picture of land that looked like ours. Instead, there were photos of gardens with visible boundaries, exquisite lawns or carefully trimmed hedges, none of which jibed with our setting. I loved our expansive meadows and the open view of the sky and the woods, and wanted our landscape to reflect their character.

It was our travels to the great public gardens in this country and abroad that eventually provided me with some useful ideas to guide my gardening efforts at home. One of the first gardens we toured was Bodnant in north Wales. This garden is known for its mild climate, its spectacular views of Mount Snowdon, and, my favorite, a steep-sided dell filled with rhododendrons and azaleas. At Bodnant I had an experience that would transform my gardening practices. After walking through the garden on winding, shrub-lined paths, I suddenly came upon a daffodil meadow. The effect of entering this flower-filled expanse after the enclosure of the shrubbery was so startling that I felt dazed. When I finally collected my wits, I remembered my meadow at home and resolved to make it "just like Bodnant."

Despite my efforts, this and some of my subsequent attempts to reproduce exactly the great garden plantings at home were not completely successful. In my Bodnant-like meadow, I planted a cheap naturalizing mix of daffodils, spacing them too far apart. Not all of them bloomed, and dandelions stole the show from those that did. Our hay-strewn meadow just never had the close-cropped, neat look of the one at Bodnant. Even less satisfying was my woodland planting of spring-flowering shrubs, which I modeled after several public gardens near Charleston, South Carolina. My version included ten perpetually stunted Exbury azaleas pining for the sun.

Undaunted, I entered upon my second phase of copying. By now I understood that the scale of the great gardens did suit our land. Bigness and openness were not, in fact, detriments to creating an attractive landscape, but I'd need to adapt what I saw to my site. At the same time, I became interested in large gardens that were surrounded by a less dramatic setting than some of the public gardens I'd first visited. The college gardens in Oxford, England, and those at nearby estates such as Rousham House, for example, seemed to parallel more closely our gently rolling farmland.

Regardless of the setting, all of these great gardens shared many similar features. Like the travel-weary tourist for whom all cathedrals look alike, I found that the details of the individual gardens blended in my mind. But the common elements of their designs became clearer. All had formal flower beds, a large lawn, a parkland of meadow and forest, naturalized daffodils, a mass planting, and water features. Once I'd identified these elements, I adapted them to fit our landscape.

Formal flower beds

At first glance, the formal flower plantings in a great garden seem beyond the scope of a home gardener. They're often surrounded by clipped boxwood hedges, adorned with statues, and terraced with elegant walls and stairs. They have, however, other characteristics that easily can be adapted to a home garden. The formal beds, composed of a colorful display of perennial flowers, are usually located near the house for ready access. If the gardens can be seen from the house, so much the better. Whether the beds are laid out geometrically or with curving edges, the flowers add a bright splash of color amidst a green expanse of lawn. The visual impact makes the formal area seem large, although it's actually quite small compared to the total amount of land of the estate.

To create an atmosphere of lush profusion, I've concentrated my new perennial borders in a few relatively restricted areas. A sheltered south-facing courtyard formed by our two barns provides a perfect niche for several beds. I've enlarged the long, skinny flower beds that I'd previously dug along the stone walls, gradually deepening them and curving their edges. In doing so, I've created a more relaxed look than that found in some of the great gardens, a look that matches our country site better. Of course, this activity has resulted in what every gardener loves to do: expand the gardens. By adding a little each year, I haven't found the work burdensome. I have learned, however, that it's wise to keep formal borders to a size that I'm able to maintain,

The gardens at Bodnant, England, (left) first provided Hogendorn with ideas for landscaping her own property. The mowed path leading from the formal border in the foreground to a parkland meadow and forest, and the mass plantings of shrubs edging the meadows, are typical features of the great gardens. In her own garden (above), a mass planting of yellow daffodils and blue lungwort creates a cheery look in a grove of maple and ash trees.

since these are the most labor-intensive part of gardening. If you have any doubts, just look at a great garden that has fallen upon hard times—the formal beds are the first to decline.

Open lawns, secret spaces
The beauty of flower beds is greatly enhanced when they're set off by a large lawn. Most American yards already contain a mowed area of considerable size, but there are still some lessons to be learned from the great estates. First, the lawn often leads to a focal point. This can be a natural feature such as a fine old tree, or a man-made one such as a gazebo. Second, and more important, not everything is open to view and immediately obvious, despite the large lawn. Enclosed areas around its edges entice the viewer to explore. The contours of the land can likewise create surprises.

Here were the solutions to my dissatisfaction with our broad, spreading lawns and meadows, which were lovely but revealed everything at once and had no points of focus. We've now made trails leading into the woodland, which attract the eyes and feet into its shelter. An opening in a stone wall along the top of a hill invites exploration. After passing through it, you suddenly see a woodland garden off to the right, full of daffodils in springtime. If a wall is lacking, outbuildings work well for hiding a special spot that can be discovered by turning a corner. Trees, bushes and fences also can block off a secret area, in contrast to the openness of a lawn.

Parkland of meadow and forest
Early in our travels I realized that the kept forest and meadow, or parkland, of the British mansions provided a good model for our property. The parkland, which comprises most of a great garden's acreage, is easily traversed on maintained trails. Brush is cleared from beneath the tree canopy, allowing the eye to move freely between the openness of the meadow and the enclosure of the forest.

We could never hope to maintain all our woods with such care, but trimming the brush under the trees at the woods' edge gives the illusion of a kept forest while requiring only a moderate amount of labor. This practice makes the woods look attractive in all seasons. Trails through the forest, which we easily maintain by picking up fallen branches twice a year and occasionally removing trees, allow for peaceful walks, as do the mowed paths through the meadows. We've tried to translate to our own land one characteristic all great gardens share: the chance to walk yourself to exhaustion always surrounded by beauty.

Meadows in our area must be mowed at least once a year or they'll become forest. To do this, we use the services of a local farmer, who takes one or two cuttings of hay from our meadows each year. Because of the labor and equipment involved, this is one of the few gardening jobs we don't do ourselves.

Naturalized daffodils
The great gardens of Europe and America often include a woodland area where the canopy of the trees has been trimmed up to accommodate a planting of flowering shrubs and bulbs beneath. After my failure to create an azalea garden here in these northern woods, I turned to the Keukenhof garden near Lisse, Holland, for my inspiration. This garden is truly a showcase for spring bulbs. Each planting forms a distinct composition separated by carefully-maintained lawns and paths, and even streams.

The meticulous care required to maintain this garden would be hard for an individual to reproduce, but I found an easy way to adapt its most appealing aspects. Instead of gravel and paved paths and bare soil beneath the bulbs, I cleared earth paths through the woods and left fallen leaves as mulch, much as I saw in the gardens of the American South. Rather than plant large masses of bulbs, especially tulips, which are characteristic of the Keukenhof garden, I planted mostly daffodils under the maple and ash trees in my woodland. I grouped them by species in separate, small clumps and interspersed them with

The clusters of spring-flowering bulbs that grace the Keukenhof garden in Holland (left) prompted the author to plant small groups of daffodils throughout her woodland (above).

Photo at left, Dianne Hogendorn; upper right, Staff

A mowed path meandering from the woods, across a meadow and to the barn, invites a walk through this parkland. The gently curving path leads visitors onward, revealing the route little by little. The meadow's mood changes seasonally, so the walks are never boring.

other flowers to accentuate them. I like the woodland garden so much that I've added plants that flower later in the season as well, such as astilbes and hostas. My woodland garden, which is about half an acre in size, has proven pleasantly easy to maintain once established. All I do is weed the paths about three or four times each year.

Mass planting

Another feature the owner of a large yard can adapt from the great gardens is mass planting, a large grouping of one kind of plant. All British estates seem to have a daffodil meadow. When allowed to spread freely, spring bulbs don't look as unsightly when the foliage dies as they would in a formal flower border. Many other flowers or shrubs also can be massed to achieve a spectacular seasonal display. These need not be unusual plants—even the most common ones look impressive when grouped in large numbers. Sissinghurst garden in England, for example, has two rectangular beds of thyme surrounded by paving, a striking sight when the purple and white flowers are in bloom.

In my own yard I have large plantings of lungwort, sedums, hostas and daylilies. This year I'm adding pink coneflowers for late-summer color. I also take advantage of flowers that spring up naturally by leaving them untouched. Our meadows are full of wildflowers in June, a mass planting of greater size and brilliance than any I could create easily.

Water features

Finally, water is an ever-present element in the great gardens, in the form of pools, rivers, fountains or waterfalls. In most cases, the gifts of nature are enhanced by human engineering. We have no standing water on our property, but we had a pinhole view of a nearby lake across an overgrown meadow. When that meadowland came up for sale, we bought and cleared it

without delay. Now our spacious lawn sweeps down toward the lake, which dominates the scene. Many properties have ponds and streams that could be emphasized in a landscaping plan. In the absence of a more imposing water view, a small pool or even a birdbath will add interesting reflections of the sky in a garden.

It's obvious that we've had to make some adjustments in copying the great gardens. We scale things down to fit with the realities of our time and economics. I don't mind working hard to create a special place, but I want to make sure it won't be so difficult to maintain that there's no time left to enjoy it. Many of our woodland trails need only to have fallen branches picked up in spring and fall. I avoid planting hedges, bushes or lawn areas that need regular trimming, as well as formal avenues that would be spoiled if one plant should die. Unpaved paths can be troublesome when they get weedy, and if you like gardening, you don't want to spend all your time caring for paths. Even with dry-laid paths you may need to lift each stone to weed out the grass that inevitably creeps out from the moist soil beneath. I've had success making paths of trampled earth in the woodland, of grass between perennial borders and in the meadows, and of sawdust in the ornamental vegetable garden. We've tried to keep our land natural-looking like the English parkland, but without the classical statues, temples and other elaborate structures that would be out of place, both aesthetically and financially, on a Maine farm. Smaller stone objects such as birdbaths and sundials look much better in our garden.

A farmer down the road once remarked to me that we have turned our once-working farm into an estate. That was a compliment, from my point of view, but I know he regretted the loss of animals. Working still goes on here, but more importantly, we've managed to set aside some time just to savor our achievements.   □

Dianne Hogendorn gardens in East Vassalboro, ME.

The Artful Garden

Sweeps of color paint an outdoor canvas

Curving paths of grass lead to island beds and wooded nooks bejeweled with colorful plants and sculptures. The artist-gardener designed his garden using the principles of repetition of color and line. (Photo taken at A on site plan on facing page.)

by Ann Champney

It was a personal vision of beauty that led Dick Meyer in 1949 to begin gardening on four shaded suburban lots in Columbus, Ohio. An artist, Dick brought a keen sense of design to everything he did, from painting and photography to needlepoint, but above all else he loved his outdoor canvas, as he called his garden. He retired from the field of commercial art when he was in his fifties so he could devote all of his energy to its ever-changing palette.

I began my commitment to the Meyer garden in 1988 when I was a horticulture student at Ohio State University. Jim Miller, a fellow horticulture student, and I were in a group touring the garden, and we volunteered to help clear some of the weeds out of Dick's lily pond. As it turned out, Dick's health was failing. He asked us to come back and help care for the garden.

After Dick died later that year, Jim and I stayed on. We have many questions that we were never able to ask Dick, but we get our answers by following his last words of gardening advice to us, "use your eye." We learned right

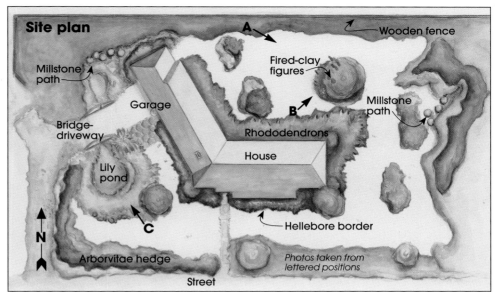

Site plan

Wooden fence

Millstone path

Fired-clay figures

A

B

Garage

Bridge-driveway

Millstone path

Rhododendrons

Lily pond

House

Hellebore border

N

C

Arborvitae hedge

Photos taken from lettered positions

Street

away that the garden would show us all the lessons in beauty that Dick so carefully worked out. That first autumn, as we were dividing irises in one of the beds, we looked up and caught sight of the red color of a nearby Virginia creeper, then saw the echoes of red Japanese maples throughout the garden, and finally spotted a distant crescendo of sunlight on a brilliant, red-painted metal sculpture at the bend of a garden path.

Frames, borders and beds

Dick framed his outdoor canvas with trees, fencing and borders. He removed some trees, limbed-up others to allow light into heavily wooded areas and planted more trees in open areas for symmetry. A curving row of arborvitae now screens the front yard from the street and forms the background for two borders. (See site plan above.) Astilbes, hostas and hardy begonias (*Begonia grandis*) grow on the protected, shady garden side, while panicums, rudbeckias, daylilies and early spring bulbs grow on the sunny, exposed, street side. A tall, wooden fence masked by evergreens and deciduous ornamentals frames the back property line, screening out neighboring homes. And the garden's backyard border is anchored by this row of tall, black-green yews, which provides a dark background for azaleas in the spring and for goldenrod (*Solidagos*), daylilies and the long, white flower spikes of bugbane (*Cimicifuga*) in late summer.

When the frame was in place, Dick used garden hose to lay out flower beds with sweeping curves—a design element that complements the rounded shapes of plants and repeats the curves of the sculptures that punctuate the garden. In one bed, a curved wooden bench under a sycamore tree provides a place to rest and to view a sculpture of an arching gazelle's head. Nearby, the linear curves of a tall, elegant urn complement the rounded shape of a yew. Urn and yew visually merge with the flowing line of the bed's edge. Dick continued the theme of curves in the garden by planting globe-shaped holly trees at the corners of the house, and

by ringing the rim of the lily pond with the rounded leaves of hostas. The curving, 8-ft. wide foundation border fronting the house is solidly planted with hellebores (*Helleborus orientalis*), an evergreen ground cover that sends up greenish white or plum flowers in late winter. From the rich, black-green hellebore foliage arise mounds of tree peonies and hardy begonias. Dick massed azaleas in borders on two sides of the house and planted a rhododendron grove on the north side. He created four curving island beds to break up the expanse of lawn in the shady backyard.

Paths and sculptures

Paths weave throughout the garden. As Dick increased the number of beds and borders, the lawn diminished, largely to grassy paths. Important elements of his design, they frame island beds and lead the eye as well as the foot. There are also narrow footpaths of other materials. One path is made of millstones and winds behind the beds in the backyard, leading to a replica of the famous Modigliani sculpture "Tete de Femme," which rises from a bed of ferns and Solomon's seal.

Sculptures are the exclamation points of Dick's garden—he used them in place of flowers to brighten shaded areas and to serve as guideposts to direct the eye from one point to another throughout the property. Suspended from an old walnut tree in the center of the back garden, a mobile in red, yellow and blue does a slow dance high above an island bed where terra cotta figures of a boy and girl kneel among Japanese painted ferns.

Illustration: Rosalind Loeb Wanke

(Above) Luminous blades of *Arundo donax variegata*, a green-and-white-striped variegated grass, and dainty, white-flowered sweet woodruff brighten a deeply shaded planting of blue-green hostas. (Below) Fired-clay figures of a boy and girl kneel among golden hostas, Japanese painted ferns and thalictrums. (Photo taken at B.)

A welcoming pool

Turning adversity to virtue, Dick transformed a low spot in front of his house into a lily pool. It is spanned by the driveway, which Dick ornamented with low wooden railings like those on an Oriental bridge, and it is surrounded by a rich tapestry of plants. In May the pink umbels (umbrella-shaped flower heads) of the aptly named umbrella plant (*Peltiphyllum peltatum*) rise high above its leaves, and Joe-Pye weed (*Eupatorium maculatum*), a moisture-loving native with broad leaves and purple flowers that bloom in late summer, shoots to great heights.

Designing with color

Dick's favorite color combination was red and chartreuse (a shade of yellow-green). He used plants with these colors to brighten shady areas and to draw the eye through the garden to achieve an illusion of greater depth or perspective. The beet red of annual coleus leaves interplanted with red-flowered astilbes stands out against the chartreuse inflorescence of *Thalictrum glaucum* and the pale green Japanese painted ferns. Hardy begonia is a signature plant of this garden, combining both colors with its chartreuse leaves and deep red stems and veining. It has colonized, spreading throughout the garden. Cardinal flower (*Lobelia cardinalis*), which possesses the most intensely red flowers, has been allowed to seed, so it brightens up the entire garden. Dick used the gold-green accents of the beautiful grass *Hakonechloa macra* 'Aureola' to light up deeply shaded areas, and he planted golden carpets of moneywort (*Lysimachia nummularia*) where it can sparkle in the sun next to emerging red tips of peony and, later, red-plumed astilbes and blue Siberian irises.

A variegated shade bed in the backyard is a delightful patchwork with a theme of chartreuse highlighted in yellow and white. Cimicifugas, a golden false cypress (*Chamaecyparis*), and the hemlock 'Gentsch White Tip', which has silver needles, preside over pulmonarias, green and yellow sedges, variegated dwarf ivy, dwarf euonymus, symphytums and *Lamium* 'Beacon Silver' and 'White Nancy'; small, gold-colored hostas are highlights.

Improving and living with soil

Careful soil preparation made it possible to grow a wide variety of plants and contributed to the garden's longevity, but it was an arduous, long-

Beneath the branches of a weeping crabapple tree, hostas and yews ring a lily pool with shades of green and blue. The driveway, which crosses the pool, is disguised as an Oriental moon bridge. (Photo taken at C.)

term effort. Dick worked wheelbarrowful after wheelbarrowful of peat moss, vermiculite and perlite into the garden's alkaline, heavy clay soil. He lowered the soil pH so profoundly that acid-loving plants such as rhododendrons still thrive where he planted them 43 years ago. Even so, we continually improve the soil—adding cottonseed meal and peat moss to acidify and break up the stubborn clay. We fertilize with a granular 6-24-24 formula and mulch with fallen leaves at the end of each growing season.

In some low-lying areas, the clay soil retains water until midsummer. Dick took full advantage of this condition by planting ostrich ferns and crested ferns, astilbes and North American burnet (*Sanguisorba canadensis*), a clump-former with fluffy, raspberry-colored, bottlebrush-shaped flowers, in marshy beds. Moisture lovers such as filipendulas, primroses, Japanese irises, foxgloves and spiderworts (*Tradescantia*) line the millstone paths. Hostas, Japanese irises, umbrella plants and buttercups planted around the lily pond also enjoy wet feet.

Gardening in shade

Most of the garden has gradually changed from damp shade to dry shade as maturing trees and other plants compete for moisture. Many of the plants that Dick used to paint his outdoor canvas reflect his increasingly sophisticated plant choices and the increasing shade of mature trees. When the garden was new, Dick grew daylilies, Asiatic and Oriental lilies, and irises. Today shade-loving hostas, ferns, thalictrums, astilbes, pulmonarias and hellebores predominate, with tree peonies, daylilies and phlox populating sunnier sites.

Dry shade necessitated a few adjustments. Building moisture-retaining raised beds has circumvented some dry-shade problems. One such bed, beneath a very old sycamore tree, is planted with golden hostas and astilbes. Its topdressing of rose-colored cobblestones maintains the garden's red and chartreuse color scheme. A raised bed under an old walnut tree in the backyard is rimmed with crumbled red lava rock to provide the red coloring to complement the

Japanese painted ferns, thalictrums, sedges and hostas growing beneath the tree. The plants in this raised bed grow happily, without a thought to juglone, a substance toxic to some plants, which is produced by the roots of walnut trees. Successful dry-shade plants that have multiplied include sedums, epimediums, lamiums and symphytum. Epimediums earn the nickname 'Barrenwort' by growing in dry-shade conditions scorned by other plants. They produce rose, yellow or white blooms in the spring. Lamiums light up dry shade with their silver- or white-blotched leaves and rose or white flowers in spring. But symphytums are probably the toughest of these ground covers—tolerating shade, wind and even drought.

The beauty that Dick Meyer created endures. And although Jim Miller and I look after Dick's garden, it remains a distinct and highly personal vision that reflects its creator. □

Ann Champney teaches perennial gardening and tends the Dick Meyer garden in Columbus, Ohio.

Planters placed for impact—Sumptuous planters packed with pink petunias and white and blue lobelias line a deck outside the author's cottage, announcing the entry into the main garden. Surrounding flowers pick up the colors in the planters and draw the eye onward.

A Design from the Heart

Growing what you love can lead to a beautiful garden

by Penny Vogel

hen I was about three, my family would visit an old couple who had the most wonderful garden I can remember. There were paths that led everywhere: to the vegetable garden, to the spring, to the beehives and then on into the woods beyond. I loved wandering these paths, surrounded by flowers that frequently grew over my head—masses of daffodils in the spring, then sweet Williams, columbines, spice pinks, Canterbury bells, foxgloves and hollyhocks. The time we spent in this wonderland was always too short, but every time I left, the old couple let me pick as many flowers as I could carry.

I'm glad to say I've had a chance to recreate the joy and wonder I felt in that garden in my own garden today. I've made a very informal cottage-style country garden: paths meander through a rainbow of flowers, and a huge variety of plants all mingle together

All photos: Susan Kahn; Illustrations: Grace Scharr

Key to planting at right

1. *Erodium chrysanthum*
2. **Broom** (*Cytisus* spp.)
3. **Pinks** (*Dianthus* 'Desmond', 'Danielle Marie')
4. **Coralbells** (*Heuchera* 'Chartreuse')
5. **Flowering tobacco** (*Nicotiana* hybrids)
6. **Shirley poppies** (*Papaver rhoeas*)
7. **Yarrow** (*Achillea* 'Moonbeam')
8. **Crocosmia** (*Crocosmia* 'Lucifer')
9. **Daylilies** (*Hemerocallis* spp.)
10. **Spike speedwell** (*Veronica spicata*)
11. **Lilies** (*Lilium* spp.)
12. **Feverfew** (*Tanacetum parthenium*)
13. **Delphiniums,** Pacific giant mix

Bright yellow color area—Eye-popping yellow and red flowers create an exuberant mood. Grouping flowers of similar colors in one area makes a bigger impact than scattering them throughout the garden.

with abandon. An exuberant garden like this one belongs with the tiny cottage my husband and I rent in a picturesque, rural setting. It's a great pleasure that my landlady and friend, Millie Kiggins, loves the garden as much as I do and lets me garden as I want.

Playing with color

Color areas—Soon after I started, I realized that the most effective areas had flowers within a limited color range; there the colors stood out and were more pleasing to the eye. Now I plant most of the garden in color areas.

Creating a new color area is easy. I simply decide on the colors to emphasize, choose plants with flowers of those colors and start planting. I try to group at least three plants of the same kind together; it makes a bigger impact and enables me to blend different groups of plants. When it's not in my budget to buy even three plants, I buy just one and propagate from it.

Working with yellow—The bright yellow area of my garden has been the easiest to develop, and it looks good from earliest spring through late fall (see photo above). There always seem to be yellow flowers in bloom; they never seem to clash, and they can be readily mixed with almost any other color. I've found that bright yellow flowers appear more hot and vibrant when they're combined with bright blue or orange-red flowers. For example, I've mixed yellow threadleaf coreopsis (*Coreopsis verticillata*) and *C.*

Pink color area—Pink candytuft flowers (foreground) are echoed by the delicate pink geraniums and pink daisy flowers of *Erigeron* 'Charity' behind. To the right of the candytuft, the blue flowers of forget-me-nots and the silvery leaves of artemisia help blend different shades of pink.

grandiflora 'Sunray' with blue delphiniums and red crocosmia. The coreopsis are low, bushy perennials with daisy flowers, the delphiniums have towering flower spikes, and the crocosmias' flower spikes poke out of grass-like leaves.

Bright yellow flowers appear more soothing when they're interspersed with lots of soft yellow, white and cream-colored flowers. I've mixed bright yellow flowers with the soft yellow ones of yarrow 'Moonshine', coreopsis 'Moonbeam', an unnamed seedling daylily and with feverfew (*Tanacetum parthenium*), which has creamy white flowers. All are perennials that grow about 2 ft. tall.

I create a transition between the bright yellow areas and the pink areas using three techniques. At the edge of the bright yellows, I plant softer yellows. Then I introduce pale blue, mauve or lavender flowers, and finally add plants with pink flowers. I also add plants with gray foliage, which are calming and blend well with just about any color (see top photo on facing page).

Success with pink—Compared to yellow flowers, pink flowers often clash with each other, making them much more difficult to combine successfully. In my garden right now, the coral-pink flowers of coralbells (*Heuchera sanguinea*) fight with the hot pink flowers of catchfly (*Lychnis viscaria*). I'll move them apart, but adding white-flowered plants can also help blend discordant shades of pink.

Some pink flowers do get along well. Candytuft (*Iberis sempervirens*), a low, mounding annual smothered with vibrant rose, pink and mauve flowers, flows smoothly through other pink flowers (see photo at left). Masses of catmint (*Nepeta mussinii*), a 1-ft. tall perennial with pale lavender-blue flowers and gray foliage, create a harmonious counterpoint to the many shades of pink.

Sources of inspiration

I'm constantly on the lookout for new combinations. Some are inspired by bouquets. For example, I make dried-flower bouquets with the flat, gold flowers of yarrow 'Coronation Gold' and the spiky purple flowers of lavender. I repeat the combination in the garden, adding yellow coreopsis or a few plants of red geum, a 1-ft. tall perennial (see photo below left).

Some of my favorite combinations happen when self-sowing plants end up together by chance. I often duplicate the combination the next season in other areas of the garden, placing the new seedlings where I want them. Self-sowing companions that I especially like are foxgloves (*Digitalis purpurea*), which bear white to bright magenta, bell-shaped flowers on tall flower stems, and fireweed (*Epilobium angustifolium*), whose rose-pink flowers sit atop 3-ft. to 5-ft. tall stalks.

Inspiration—Inspired by a bouquet, the author combined the spiky flowers of two lavenders ('Hidcote' on left; 'Munsted' on right), which spill over the edge of the bed, with the dome-shaped gold flowers of yarrow 'Coronation Gold' just behind.

Planters placed for impact

Visitors to my garden are always surprised and delighted by the view that appears when they step up to the deck outside my cottage door. Here they are greeted by planter boxes overflowing with hot pink petunias and lobelias, whose small flowers in white and shades of blue freely cover 6-in. high plants (see photo on p. 90). These easy-to-grow annuals also spill out of nearby window boxes.

Temporarily stopping to feast their eyes on the lush planters, visitors soon look past them down a flower-lined path that welcomes them into the garden. Stately blue delphiniums and pink shrub roses just beyond the deck carry forward the blue and pink of the planters. On a clear day, the distant snow-capped peak of Mt. Hood becomes visible beyond the end of the path.

Paths that lead to surprises

I still love meandering paths, just as I did as a child. They beckon me to follow. When you round the corner at the end of the path leading from the deck into my garden, a flush of pink and lavender flowers greets you, in contrast to the bright yellow and red gypsy colors you've just passed by. Further along, a bench invites you to sit. Or you might be enticed to continue up the main path, where you'll come to our village of birdhouses, all handcrafted by Millie. (For photos of the birdhouses, see the back cover of this issue. To purchase a birdhouse, contact Millie Kiggins, 26661 South Kinzy Rd., Estacata, OR 97023, 503-630-7360.) These birdhouses are special because they're miniature buildings, such as an inn, a general store and even a tiny chicken coop. Beyond them, a slight climb through

Transition area—Soft yellow and lavender flowers, with an accent of red, ease the transition between the bright yellow area and a pink area. A birdbath delights birds and onlookers alike.

a small, serene grove of fir trees leads to a small church that Millie built in memory of her grandparents, who originally bought this place.

Almost every morning, from late winter until late fall, cup of coffee in hand, I walk through my garden. With the sun coming up over the mountain and the birds singing, it seems like a little piece of heaven. As winter ends, I watch my garden come back to life, discovering the first bulbs pushing through the earth, noting the first hint of fresh green growth on perennials, or savoring the smell of the first violets. As summer progresses, I sit at the picnic table and just enjoy the view. ▪

Penny Vogel's young, lush garden in Estacata, Oregon, draws garden tours from Portland and surrounding areas.

A path leads to surprises—The main path into the author's garden winds into the heart of the bright yellow flower area, with a view of the foothills of Mt. Hood in the distance. A low mound of *Corydalis lutea* punctuates the foreground.

Index

A

Annuals, overgrowing for more flowers, 81
Arbors, in garden design, 45
Ashmun, Barbara, on designing with beds and borders, 28-32

B

Beaubaire, Nancy, on edible landscaping, 62-64
Beds, flower:
    formal, on large estates, 83-84
    in garden design, 81
    island, 28-32
Boden, Anne, on designing a flower border, 24-27
Borders, flower:
    designing, 24-27
    in garden design, 81
    with island beds, 28-32
Brick, as design material, 65, 66, 67, 68

C

Carney, Nancy, on crowding perennials, 54-57
Champney, Ann, on artful garden, 86-89
Color, in garden design, 10-11, 26, 33-36, 58-61, 76-77, 79, 82, 91-92
Containers, for small yard, 67
Courtyard, garden, 78-81
Crawford, Bruce, on wooden entry walkway, 70-73

D

Drotar, David Lee, on beginner's design method, 19-23
Ducsik, Andrew, on principles of Gertrude Jekyll, 33-37

E

Entryway, wooden walk, 70-73

F

Fences, in garden design, 9, 47, 48
Flowers, for long-blooming garden, 58-61
Foliage:
    in garden design, 35-36
    See also Texture.
Fragrance:
    as focus for garden, 74-77
    in garden design, 79

G

Garden design:
    with beds and borders, 28-32
    computer-aided, 24-25
    cottage garden, 90-93
    of cottage-style border, 24-25
    courtyard, 78-81
    with crowded perennials, 54-57
    five principles of, 8-11
    with food plants, 62-64
    with garden rooms, 65-69
    Japanese, five principles of, 46-49
    of large estates, 82-85
    memories as inspiration for, 16-18
    for season-long color, 58-61
    site analysis for, 12-15
    for small space, 74-77
    stake-and-cord method for, 27
    walled garden, 72-73
    See also Landscape design. Landscaping.
Gardening, in dry shade, 54-57, 89
Grese, Robert E., on design principles of Jens Jensen, 38-41

H

Hogendorn, Dianne, on landscaping a large property, 82-85
Hooker, Will, on intuitive garden design, 16-18
Horton, Orene, on garden rooms, 65-69

J

Japanese garden, design principles of, 46-49
Jekyll, Gertrude:
    using principles of, 33-37
    work of, 36
Jensen, Jens, landscape design by, 38-41

L

Landscape design:
    beginner's method for, 19-23
    Prairie School of, 38-41
    See also Garden design. Landscaping.
Landscaping:
    applying ideas from great estates, 82-85
    edible, books on, 64
    edible, discussed, 62-64
    with mass plantings, 85
    with native plants, 42-45
    with naturalized flowers, 84-85
    nature as inspiration for, 38-41
    See also Garden design. Landscape design.
Lappin, Jane E., on courtyard garden, 78-81
Lawns, open, on large estates, 84
Licht, Avis Rappoport, on designing for a small side yard, 74-77
Light, natural, in landscape design, 39-40, 41
Lutyens, Edwin, work of, 36

M

Map, site, developing, 12-15
Meadows, on large estates, 84, 85
Meyer, Dick, artful garden of, 86-89

O

Ornamentals, edible, 62-64

P

Parks, Joe, on garden paths, 50-53
Paths:
    design principles for, 51-52
    in garden design, 8-9, 47, 49, 50-53, 93
    grass, 81, 83, 84, 85
    materials for, 52-53
    stone, 74, 75
    wooden entryway, 70-73
Patios, stone, 74, 75, 77
Perennials:
    for long-blooming garden, 54-57, 58-61
    for mature, shady garden, 86-89
    overgrowing for more flowers, 81
Planters:
    in entry walkway, 70, 71, 72
    in garden design, 90, 93
Plants:
    food, designing with, 62-64
    native, for garden design, 42-45
    for shade, 54-57
    stalwart, for new beds and borders, 31-32
    for sun, 56
    for wet soil, 56
Plumer, Cathyann, on developing a site map, 12-15
Pools, lily, in garden design, 82
Prairie School design, discussed, 38-41

S

Sawyers, Claire, on Japanese garden design, 46-49
Sculptures, in garden design, 81
Shrubs, as background in garden design, 9
Smaus, Robert, on design principles, 8-11
Smith, John W. (Jack), on continuous flower color, 58-61
South Carolina, small garden with rooms, 65-69
Stark, Judith, on native plant landscape, 42-45
Steps, for entry walkway, 71, 72
Symmetry, in garden design, 79-81

T

Terraces:
    council-ring, 40
    hillside, in garden design, 74-77
Texture:
    in garden design, 11, 26, 79
    See also Foliage.

V

Vogel, Penny, on informal cottage garden, 90-93

W

Walkways. *See* Paths.
Walls:
    in garden design, 48
    retaining, dry-laid bluestone, 71-72
    retaining, granite-riprap, 74, 77
Wisconsin, native plant landscape, 42-45

The 21 articles in this book originally appeared in *Fine Gardening* magazine.
The date of first publication, issue number and page numbers for each article are given below.

If you enjoyed this book, you're going to love our magazine.

A year's subscription to *Fine Gardening* brings you the kind of hands-on information you found in this book, and much more. In issue after issue—six times a year—you'll find articles on nurturing specific plants, landscape design, fundamentals and building structures. Expert gardeners will share their knowledge and techniques with you. They will show you how to apply their knowledge in your own backyard. Filled with detailed illustrations and full-color photographs, *Fine Gardening* will inspire you to create and realize your dream garden!

To subscribe, just fill out one of the attached subscription cards or call us at 1-800-888-8286. And as always, your satisfaction is guaranteed, or we'll give you your money back.

Taunton
MAGAZINES
for fellow enthusiasts

BUSINESS REPLY MAIL
FIRST-CLASS MAIL   PERMIT NO. 6   NEWTOWN CT

POSTAGE WILL BE PAID BY ADDRESSEE

FINE GARDENING®

63 S MAIN STREET
PO BOX 5507
NEWTOWN CT 06470-9877

Taunton
MAGAZINES
for fellow enthusiasts

BUSINESS REPLY MAIL
FIRST-CLASS MAIL   PERMIT NO. 6   NEWTOWN CT

POSTAGE WILL BE PAID BY ADDRESSEE

FINE GARDENING®

63 S MAIN STREET
PO BOX 5507
NEWTOWN CT 06470-9877